Thomson McElrath

A Press Club Outing

A trip across the continent to attend the first convention of the International

League of Press Clubs

Thomson McElrath

A Press Club Outing
A trip across the continent to attend the first convention of the International League of Press Clubs

ISBN/EAN: 9783337147266

Printed in Europe, USA, Canada, Australia, Japan

Cover: Foto ©Andreas Hilbeck / pixelio.de

More available books at **www.hansebooks.com**

A Press Club
Outing.

* ☙ *

A trip ▪ ·
Across the Continent to attend the First Convention
of the International League of Press Clubs.

BY

Thomson P. McElrath,

Historian of the Trip.

* ☙ *

NEW YORK:
International League of Press Clubs.
1893.

-

THE JAMES KEMPSTER PRINTING COMPANY,
117-119-121 Liberty Street,
New York.

*T*HIS brief record of a very agreeable journey from the Atlantic to the Pacific and back again, had its origin in a resolution adopted by the Convention of the International League of Press Clubs, in session in the rooms of the San Francisco Press Club, January 14th, 1892. The official report of the proceedings of that Convention refers to the subject as follows:

"On the motion of Mr. Welshons, of Pittsburgh, Major T. P. McElrath, of New York, was elected Historian of the League, to prepare a book descriptive of the California trip; with the President and Secretary as an advisory committee, to arrange for the publication of the work."

The preparation of the book has been attended with delays and hindrances both potent and unavoidable, for which the writer alone is responsible, and for which he asks the friendly indulgence of his fellow travelers. Similar lenity he trusts they will accord to the book itself, accepting it rather in the light of a completed task than in that of a finished production. It is too little a pudding to contain many plums. Its purpose, as the writer conceives it, will be fully served if it proves adequate to keep alive the delightful personal associations connected with the three memorable weeks of sunshine and pleasure enjoyed by the Press Club Delegates to the San Francisco Convention.

PREFACE.

At a public meeting of the International League of Press Clubs in the Powell Street Opera House, San Francisco, on the evening of January 15th, 1892, more than twenty letters from the most eminent and successful men in journalism and literature were read, and were received with cordial applause by the large audience. Extracts from a few of them will give an accurate idea of the tenor of their expressions. Mr. George William Curtis wrote: "The general objects of the League of Press Clubs, as I understand them, seem to me worthy of the most zealous promotion. I see no good reason why the courtesy of the press should not be as distinguished as its independence and vigor." Mr. Chester S. Lord wrote: "I approve most assuredly of the objects and purposes which have led to the organization of the International League, and I wish the association every possible success." Hon. Theodore Barth wrote from Berlin: "Unfortunately, my duties as a member of the German Reichstag, just now in session, do not permit the acceptance of the invitation. This I regret so much more because, in my opinion, the idea of uniting representatives of the press in international congresses is a very happy one. In view of the far-reaching and constantly growing influence of the press, its representatives can do more than legislators and diplomats for maintaining friendly relations among nations, towards removing nativistic prejudices, for exercising international justice and fostering especially interests which are common to all mankind." Colonel John A. Cockerill wrote: "I believed in the League from the outset. The best results must

7

flow from the establishment of the closer brotherhood among the press workers of both hemispheres." Dr. Max Nordeau wrote from Paris: "I am at heart with you. I highly appreciate your noble aim, and think it a most happy idea to unite all the press workers of the world in one great brotherhood." Hon. Amos J. Cummings wrote: "I hope that the International League of Press Clubs will finally include delegates from press clubs in every State in the United States where a daily newspaper is published." The other letters were similar in their endorsements of the plans and purposes of the organization of the newspaper workers of the world. These quotations are made for the reason that the writers represent the various phases of practical and successful journalism.

There has always been a need of a general association of the people who write and edit newspapers, but one great obstacle stood in the way of those who tried to carry the matter to a substantial result. Newspaper men are bothered with hard things called opinions, and when the matter is close to their own interests the opinion is apt to be somewhat narrow, which, of course, goes to show that the newspaper men are painfully like the rest of their race. So, while the journalism of the world has been the evangel and the messenger boy of civilization, and has spread progress and culture and humanity until its scope has measured to the limit of human achievement, with all the widening possibilities of life itself, the newspaper men, as a profession, have not done what they could have done to get together and to receive the benefits that must always come from association. The reasons for this are many, and all are sufficient. In the first place, the bees in the hive are busy bees, always at work making honey—or the other thing—and with few spare moments for assembling under the roses to discuss co-operative industry and organized courtesy. Then, too, the different swarms have shown a great fondness for swarming by themselves without even the formality of fraternal greetings to the other swarms. And so it has gone on until the International League of Press Clubs has opened a way along which all may go.

There are numerous organizations of editors and publishers in this and other countries, and all are useful, but they are organizations of representatives of newspapers. The League differs from them in that it binds together the associations of newspaper men. It represents the journalists as individuals rather than the newspapers as institutions. It is more social in its ambition, and "its objects," to quote its Constitution, "are to bring into close and friendly relations the press clubs of the world, and promote a more fraternal and helpful feeling among its members." It thus antagonizes none of the other organizations, but invites the favor and co-operation of all. The desire, especially, is to organize the men and women of the daily press more thoroughly. Press Clubs with us are modern. They are the out-growth of the new conditions in journalism. As they multiplied and became greater in membership and more important in material prosperity than all the other Press Clubs in the world, they felt the wisdom of a closer communion of interests and began to discuss means by which mutual advantages could be secured. About ten years ago the project of a national association was mooted. Shortly afterwards the New York Press Club sent out circulars calling for a meeting of representatives of all the Press Clubs of the country. Differences between the East and West defeated the enterprise and it was not until a few years ago that it was revived. Mr. Thomas J. Keenan, Jr., then Secretary, and afterwards President, of the Pittsburgh Press Club, entered into correspondence with the Clubs of Canada and the United States, and the outcome of his work was a formal invitation to "the journalistic organizations of the United States, Canada, the City of Mexico, and the capital cities of Europe and South America, to send delegates to a Convention to be held in Pittsburgh, on January 27th, 1891, for the purpose of organizing an International Association of Press Clubs."

Twenty-three clubs were represented in the Convention. The visitors were royally entertained. In the three days the League was born, christened and matured, and Mr. Keenan was unanimously elected its first President. The merits of the movement were briefly: The association of the organizations of the newspaper men and newspaper women of the world; the interchangeable credentials that admitted the member of one club to all clubs of the League; the mutual assistance and encouragement of League members, and the general purpose to give the profession, or calling, as you wish, the broadest benefits of organization. The League met with immediate favor, and the proof of its usefulness is found in the fact that since it was established the press clubs in this country have increased nearly one hundred per cent. in number, and more than one hundred per cent. in membership. The coming in of the German Press Clubs, and many of the Women Press Clubs, had a decided effect upon the life of the new organization.

In the pages which follow, Major McElrath tells most delightfully the story of a wonderful journey. The League had been invited to various cities, but San Francisco's offer of sunshine and flowers in January won the overwhelming favor of the Convention. For months previous to the opening of 1892, the Board of Governors was holding meetings in New York, shaping the affairs of the League and completing the arrangements for the transcontinental tour. The marvels of California's hospitality, the constant newness of scene and incident, and the beauty and the glory of it all, are described by Major McElrath. But, outside of the entertainment, much was done by the delegates representing Press Clubs in nearly twenty States of the country, and indirectly representing thousands of newspaper workers. Especially important was the inauguration of a scheme to establish a home for aged and infirm journalists. The attention that the trip attracted can be inferred from the fact that more than four hundred columns of matter was written about it in the newspapers, including reports of the speeches, which have been omitted from this otherwise faithful narrative because it was desirable to limit the book to one volume and not to publish it on the instalment plan.

Of course, the League is not old enough to be judged as an international organization. Its career thus far is mainly experimental, but that there is need of it is evident. It represents the better aspirations of a calling that has the leadership of thought and progress as its destiny. There is no evolution more remarkable than that which is going on in journalism. Already the advance has been beyond every expectation, not only in methods and resources but in men and manners. Times have changed since the days when ministers were hauled up before their brothers and tried for making and selling whiskey, not because they made and sold whiskey, but because the whiskey was bad. Times have changed since the judge adjourned the court to see the elephant swim the river, and since drunkenness was regarded as a gentlemanly indulgence among the members of the bar. And times have changed since genius drank beer and smoked pipes in cellars and attics and made impecuniosity a cardinal virtue. The newspaper man of to-day is as well trained and as well educated as his professional contemporary in the pulpit or at the bar. He is no longer a Bohemian; he is one of the hardest of the world's workers, and a practical citizen. Occasionally he becomes a plutocrat; sometimes he is a member of the Cabinet, or a minister

11

to a foreign court; he is found in the House of Representatives and in the Senate; he permeates all the departments of literature—but, generally, and at his best, he is the ever-busy, ever-thoughtful, ever-anxious factor of news-collecting and news-editing—the historian of his times—the educator of his generation, and a right good fellow, who has his share of the virtues and the frailties of humanity. Times, too, have changed since the newspapers were published in dingy buildings amidst darkness and dust. Now, the buildings rise as far toward Heaven as they can get, and stand as achievements of architecture and as wonders for the special delight of country subscribers. This development is confined to no section; it is going on everywhere. The largest newspaper building in America is west of the Mississippi River, and the Pacific coast rivals the old established papers of the East in great performances of news-gathering. While this country has distanced history and outdone the earth in its marvelous development, its newspapers have multiplied nine times more rapidly than its population, and their value has increased sixteen times faster than the national wealth. Last, but not least, the census gentleman is kind enough to inform us that of all the professions journalism is, on the average, the best paid. Considering these things, it is not too much to look forward to the time when the newspaper men shall have a general organization that will command the attention and the respect and the serious consideration of the world.

The League is young yet, and its plans and purposes are only partly understood, but even in this stage of its development it has been an influence for good, and has given a promise of usefulness that has more than fulfilled the hopes of those who were most active in organizing it. The extension of the League to all parts of newspaperdom will necessarily be slow, because many countries are without press clubs. But they will come in time. Those of us who want immediate results should look at the history of other professions. It took the doctors a great many years to establish their medical congress. Bar associations were the outgrowth of almost interminable efforts and discussions among the lawyers. Pan-church conferences are as old as the dogmas in theory, but they are extremely modern in fact. Science debated and struggled a long time before its representatives met in international councils. The Press League is less than three years old, but its strength has been splendidly seen in the growth of press clubs and the evident desire for better organization among newspaper men. Its real work has hardly begun, and its full advantages cannot be appreciated until it has become truly international in its scope and membership. When that point is reached it will be one of the most powerful organizations on earth. It is easy to smile at such optimism, but is there any one who honestly doubts that journalism, if it is not now, is sure to be the greatest factor, if not the greatest force, of civilization? Every day the world is living and moving more and more in its newspapers. Every day the newspapers are more and more absorbing the thought and directing the activities of mankind.

It is not claimed that the League represents all journalism. But it would like to represent it. It is a candidate for that high honor. It is a move which earnest men and women have made, and they desire to see their work taken up and advanced until it reaches to all the corners of the earth. It would be a happy satisfaction to mention the names of those who have been most active in the labors that have brought the League to its present position, but all the delegates and officers have cordially co-operated, and this is not a directory, but a preface which should have been written by a more important person than an ex-vice-president.

LYNN R. MEEKINS.

BALTIMORE, MARCH 15TH, 1893.

❧

" They rested there, escaped awhile
    From cares that wear the life away,
To eat the lotus of the Nile
    And drink the poppies of Cathay."

❧

A Story of *fruit, flowers and frost; of sleet and snow, and summer softness; of snow-capped mountains and valleys of sempiternal verdure; of ice-locked streams and sea bathing in midwinter; of royal hospitalities enjoyed while loitering on the sunny shore of the Pacific, and literary enterprise maintained at highest railway speed, among the snowy crests of the Rockies; of never-wearying charms of feminine sweetness and melody, and never-ceasing iterations of speech-making men; these and other points of close resemblance and startling contrast I am called upon to describe briefly, in a narrative of*

· · a Railroad Journey from · ·
New York to San Francisco
●·●·● and Return ●·●·●·●

THE GRAND CENTRAL STATION · NEW YORK.

Chapter I.

❧

❧

HERE was a jolly gathering of men and women connected with the newspaper craft in the Grand Central Station, in New York City, on the morning of Wednesday, January 6th, 1892. Outside, the streets were rapidly whitening under the first heavy snowfall of the winter, and the sky was black with lowering clouds. It was a disagreeable day for outdoor avocations. But in the passenger room of the New York Central and Hudson River Railroad on that eventful morning the state of the atmosphere was not a subject for even casual discussion. As the party arrived, singly or in couples, cordial greetings were exchanged, while the snow was brushed and shaken from overcoat and mantle, and all local considerations were ignored in the enthusiasm of joyous expectancy that illuminates the spirits of people starting from home in the quest of pleasure. The object of this gathering of dames and knights of quill and pencil was to attend the first annual Convention of the International League of Press Clubs, which was appointed to be held in San Francisco on January 13th. A year previously a similar excursion, on a smaller scale, had been made by delegates from twenty-three Press Clubs of the East and the West to the City of Pittsburgh, where, in the intervals of a royal

17

entertainment, to which the whole population of that enterprising
city seemed to contribute, there was organized a League, framed
to comprise in its membership all the Press Clubs of the world.
It was a charming initiation of a beneficent enterprise, of whose
possible scope prediction would as yet be futile. Several of those
who attended that earlier Convention were among the present
party, but the large feminine representation in the latter was an
innovation, growing naturally out of one of the League's pet
theories concerning the intellectual equality of the sexes. As the
membership is open equally to women of the press as to men, the
committee having charge of the preparations for the San Francisco
Convention authorized each delegate to invite his wife, or, in
default of such incumbrance, his best girl, to accompany him. The
advantage of this arrangement was manifest from the outset,
particularly in the case of the married delegates, as it positively
insured the presence of the better half of each domestic establishment represented, and on an occasion of this kind only the best
was desirable. The persons who set out from New York, and who
joined the party on the route, and the Press Clubs to which they
respectively were credited, were the following:

NEW YORK PRESS CLUB:

William Berri, Chairman, *Brooklyn Standard-Union*; Charles W. Price, *Electrical
Review*; W. R. Worrall, *Mail and Express*; Major T. P. McElrath, *American
Analyst*; J. I. Charlouis, *The School Journal*; George F. Lyon, *Law Journal*; Thos.
H. Evans, New York representative *Chicago Tribune* and *San Francisco Chronicle*;
Alfred E. Pearsall, *Commercial Advertiser*; E. B. Phelps, *The Club*; Chas. H.
George, New York correspondent *Baltimore American*; Samuel C. Austin, *Asso-
ciated Press*; Marshall P. Wilder, *Sunday Advertiser*; W. N. Penney, *United Press*.

Guests—Mrs. William Berri, Mrs. Chas. W. Price, Mrs. W. R. Worrall, Mrs. T. P.
McElrath, Mrs. J. I. Charlouis, Mrs. Geo. F. Lyon, Mrs. Thos. H. Evans, Master
"Tom" Evans, Mr. W. C. K. Wilde, Mrs. Frank Leslie-Wilde, Miss Mattison,
Miss Kellogg, Miss Cottrell, Miss Kate Field, Dr. A. S. Hunter and wife, Miss
Elita Proctor Otis, Mr. Foster Coates, Mr. M. H. Brown, Mr. G. H. Lowerre,
Mr. J. Seaver Page, Mr. J. C. Yager and wife, Mr. M. C. Roach.

THE NEW YORK PRESS CLUB DELEGATES.

W. H. Worrall,	W. N. Penney,	J. L. Charlouis,	C. H. George,
	T. P. McElrath,	William Berri,	Chas. W. Price,
Geo. F. Lyon,	M. P. Wilder,	A. E. Pearsall,	T. H. Evans.

BOSTON PRESS CLUB:

J. C. Morse, J. S. Keeler, W. C. Grout, *Herald*; W. V. Alexander, *Transcript*; E. J. Carpenter, *Advertiser*; William B. Smart, *Post*; Thos. F. Anderson, *Globe*. Mr. Anderson, though a member of the Governing Board of the League, was unfortunately compelled to leave the party at Chicago.

Guests—Miss Maria Parloa, Miss Helen Chamberlain.

BUFFALO PRESS CLUB:

Byron R. Newton, *News*; Eugene J. Fleury, *Express*.

GERMAN PRESS CLUB, NEW YORK:

Dr. John Friederich, *Americanische Schweizer Zeitung*.

NEW YORK WOMANS' PRESS CLUB:

Miss M. V. Lewis. Miss Lewis joined the party in San Francisco and accompanied it on the three days' trip to Del Monte and San Jose.

CHICAGO GERMAN PRESS CLUB:

Emil Hoechster and wife.

CLEVELAND WOMEN'S PRESS CLUB:

Mrs. Elroy M. Avery.

GRAND RAPIDS PRESS CLUB:

E. B. Fisher. W. B. Weston, of the Governing Board, joined at San Francisco.

CANTON, O., PRESS CLUB:

T. K. Albaugh, *Democrat*, and Mrs. Judge Albaugh.

MILWAUKEE GERMAN PRESS CLUB:

Julius Muehle and wife.

BALTIMORE JOURNALISTS' CLUB:

L. R. Meekins, Vice-President, and Mrs. Meekins; John S. Stillman, *Baltimore American*.

N. E. WOMEN'S PRESS ASSOCIATION, BOSTON:

Mrs. Lulu S. Upham, *Gazette*.

PACIFIC WOMEN'S PRESS ASSOCIATION, SAN FRANCISCO:

Miss A. E. Knapp, *Morning Call*; Mrs. E. T. Y. Parkhurst, *California Magazine*.

PITTSBURGH PRESS CLUB:

President T. J. Keenan, Jr., *Press*; Geo. H. Welshons, *Times*; Wm. H Davis, *Commercial Gazette*; L. D. Bancroft, *Dispatch*.
Guests—Mrs. Welshons, Mrs. Cameron, Miss Keenan.

PHILADELPHIA PRESS CLUB:

T. Henry Martin, *Item*, and wife.

READING PRESS CLUB:

John B. Dampman, *Herald*, and wife.

SYRACUSE PRESS CLUB:

E. H. O'Hara, *Herald*; S. G. Lapham, of the Governing Board, *Courier*.

SOUTHERN R. I. PRESS CLUB:

Irving Watson, H. F. True.

ST. PAUL PRESS CLUB:

Julius A. Schmahl, *News*, joined at Chicago; C. H. Lineau, San Francisco.

NAT'L ORG'N GERMAN-AMERICAN JOURNALISTS AND AUTHORS:

Arthur Koenig, Milwaukee, joined at Chicago; M. Greenblatt, San Francisco.

ILLINOIS WOMEN'S PRESS ASSOCIATION:

Mrs. Frances E. Owens, Miss Belle L. Gorton, Miss Mary Allen West.

TOLEDO PRESS CLUB:

P. C. Boyle, *Commercial*, wife and daughter; M. P. Murphy, *Bee*.

SAN FRANCISCO PRESS CLUB:

Hugh Hume, T. T. Williams, M. H. de Young, H. M. Tod, Theo. F. Bonnet.

After the hurried farewells had been uttered, the train, at 10.30 A. M., drew out from the depot, seven Wagner palace coaches bearing a hundred persons with hearts full of cheerful anticipation, and leaving on the platform a large group of envying friends. The train, specially provided for this excursion, and the first of its kind that ever crossed the continent from Atlantic to Pacific, deserves detailed description, which will be given at a later period in this narrative. Of the journey to Chicago, that being an affair of every-day experience, little need be said, except that it was one of uninterrupted jollity. The view through the windows of the storm that raged continuously, and the fleeting glimpses of the snow-enveloped landscape, only served to heighten the sense of enjoyment as the luxuriously appointed Wagner palace cars were whirled smoothly and swiftly along the shores of the Hudson and Mohawk Rivers. At Albany, Syracuse and Buffalo, guests and delegates from local clubs and remoter points joined the party. Canada was traversed in the night, but the steadily increasing force of the storm caused so great a delay that instead of reaching

THE SPECIAL WAGNER TRAIN CROSSING THE NIAGARA RIVER.

Chicago at 9.45 on Thursday morning, as had been expected, it was after three o'clock in the afternoon when the train pulled up at that city.

Chicago was found to be particularly windy that day, and, owing to the storm, it was also in a nebulous condition that effectually concealed it from view. A special train was in waiting, under charge of a committee representing the Chicago Press Club and the Exposition management, with Major Moses P. Handy in charge, and the newspaper guests were speedily whisked to the Exposition grounds, on the shore of Lake Michigan, where they

THE WIVES OF THE NEW YORK DELEGATES.

MRS. CHA. W. PRICE.   MRS. WILLIAM BERRI.
MRS. T. H. EVANS,   MRS. J. J. CHALLONER,   MRS. T. P. McLEAN
MRS. G. F. LYON,   MRS. W. H. WORRALL.

received a mass of valuable information, verbally and in printed shape, regarding the majestic buildings which they were told were in progress of construction all around them. But of those building operations hardly anything could be seen rain, snow, sleet and smoke effectually covering them— to the manifest chagrin of the local committee, who were indefatigable in their efforts to make amends for the shortcomings, or overdoings, of the elements. The unavoidable delay the travelers had experienced was disappointing, not only on account of curtailing the projected visit to the city, but by its interference with the arrangements that had been made for the party's entertainment by the committee. However, the only thing to do was to make the best of the situation and to see and learn as much as possible in the short time allowed them, and, accordingly, when the tour of the Exposition grounds was reported to have been completed, the delegates were whirled by rail back to Chicago, and then by carriage to the *Herald* Building, where the editor and proprietor, Col. Scott, had an elegant luncheon waiting for them. After this repast, the first, by the way, of a long series of similar entertainments, the visitors proceeded to inspect the splendid newspaper establishment in which they had received such a cordial welcome, beginning with the composing and stereotyping rooms on the sixth floor, and ending with the press room in the basement. The general verdict was one of unqualified admiration, the building being, probably, as Col. Scott claimed, the most complete newspaper office in America, and therefore in the world. While still in the composing room, the proprietor addressed a few words of welcome to his guests, to which Mr. Keenan responded in terms of appropriate compliment. The compositors of the office and the guests were attentive listeners. It was at this point that the speech-making feature of the journey received an impulse that kept it in active operation by day and night for the following twenty-four days, and across fully eight thousand miles of American soil.   Mr. Keenan was followed by Dr. Bedloe, of Philadelphia, then recently returned on leave from his consular duties in Amoy, China, Miss Kate Field, of Washington, Mr. J. Seaver Page, of New York, Mrs. Frank Leslie-Wilde, Mr. William Wilde, of London, England, and Messrs. Berri, Evans, Wilder and Pearsall, of the New York Press Club.   On parting with the hospitable host of the *Herald*

THE AUDITORIUM- CHICAGO.

the Chicago Press Club was visited. Col. J. M. Bundy welcomed the party, expressing regret for the detention that had disarranged the Club's plans for entertainment, and urging a repetition of the visit under more propitious skies on the return Eastward.   The president of the club, Wm. A. Taylor, in a few friendly words, wished the delegates a safe and pleasant journey to the Pacific slope and home again; and brief addresses were likewise made by Messrs. Hall and Almy, of the Chicago Press Club, which were replied to by Messrs. Keenan and Foster Coates.   The delegates were then invited to attend the theatres as guests of the Chicago Press Club, which some accepted, others preferring to while away the evening at the Auditorium, where the annual Charity Ball was to be held.   At 11.30 the cars were again taken.   Mr. Roach, of the New York Central Railroad, was compelled to leave the party at this point in order to return to New York.   The circumstance caused general regret, but Mr. Roach's mantle fell gracefully upon the shoulders of General Western Passenger Agent W. B. Jerome, of the same company, who joined the party at Chicago and remained with it in charge of all railroad arrangements until the train reached Detroit on its return, twenty-three days later.

Friday morning found us speeding merrily along on the Chicago & North Western Railroad. The sky was grey and the sunshine had a chilled look, especially after one of the train hands had passed through the cars with the information that the mercury registered ten degrees below zero. We were now doing some fast traveling. The run of 503 miles from Chicago to Omaha was made in thirty-five minutes less than the schedule time arranged for our special train, and was one of the very fastest ever made on that road. The country was a level treeless prairie and elicited great admiration from the tenderfeet of the excursion who had never been consciously before on a genuine prairie. The educational feature of the journey was thus entered upon at the rate of between thirty and forty miles an hour. The forenoon was passed by the ladies in the interchange of various social and sociable attentions, while the men for the most part devoted themselves to exploring and testing the varied resources of the buffet car. At 2 P. M., after crossing the Missouri at Council Bluffs, the train pulled up at Omaha, where a joint committee of the Omaha Board of Trade and the Press Club were in waiting at the depot with carriages, and a few minutes later, after escaping from a

THE OMAHA BEE BUILDING.

photographer's hands, the delegates were standing in the spacious court of the Omaha *Bee* office, listening to cheering words of welcome from the enterprising owner of the establishment, Col. Edward

Rosewater. The building in which we were entertained is claimed to cover more square feet of surface than any other newspaper edifice in the world, and it certainly is a splendid as well as a spacious establishment. It is built of granite, and is eight stories high, enclosing a large square court covered over with glass, thus insuring light to every apartment. From its lofty roof an extended view was obtained of the city, which impressed all who inspected it from that point as being the home of a remarkably enterprising and energetic people. Broad, well paved streets were lined with rows of magnificent structures, and traversed in all directions with cable and electric railroads. On every side were bustle and business activity. The welcoming addresses having been appropriately responded to by the travelers, the entire party were rapidly raised by elevator to the Press Club rooms on the upper floor of the building, where an hour was charmingly spent in conversation. A tidy lunch was served, to which ample justice was done, and the punch that washed it down is still fondly talked of by the New York delegates. At four o'clock we re-embarked and were under way again towards the Pacific. That evening on the train was marked by one of the characteristic incidents of the trip, a feature that probably had never before had its counterpart. After dinner Mr. J. C. Yager, of the Wagner Company, had the waiters remove all the tables from the dining car and replace them with camp chairs, produced from some place of storage whose location was one of the many permanent mysteries of the journey. Everybody thereupon repaired to that car and spent the evening in a most enjoyable manner, listening to addresses and recitations by Mr. J. Seaver Page, Foster Coates, Marshall P. Wilder, Mr. Willie Wilde, and to some excellent vocalization, of which our musical leader, Pearsall, with the stentorian lungs, was the manager and conductor.

What the visiting party did not learn concerning the City of Denver, the Queen City of the Plains, is not likely to be acquired by newspaper writers of the present generation. By the admirable arrangements of the Committee of Reception an opportunity was afforded the Eastern travelers to do up that city in exhaustive style, or as nearly so as was practicable within the compass of a single day and evening. The train arrived at the Denver depot at 10.35 A. M. on Saturday, January 9th, and the excursionists were welcomed by representatives of the local newspapers, the Chamber of Commerce, the Real Estate Exchange, and the railroad companies that center at that important city. The strong bond of interest existing between the manipulators of rates and traffics, pools, and short and long hauls, was shown by the warm interest taken in the excursionists by the railroad men. Among those who greeted the newcomers were General Ticket Agent Ady, of the Union Pacific; S. K. Hooper, General Passenger Agent of the Rio Grande; Assistant Passenger Agent Wadleigh, of the same line; C. G. Burkhardt, of the North-western; City Passenger Agent Erbb, of the Union Pacific; Commodore Trufant, Superintendent of the Union Depot; J. P. Flynn, C. H. Titus, Editor Arkins and others. Members of the Chamber of Commerce and the Denver Real Estate Exchange were: S. M. Allen, Biddle Reeves, R. E. Gurley, B. L. Sholtz, John Crawford and L. M. Townsend, of the Interior Land and Improvement Company, an old newspaper man of New York. The Reception Committee had everything arranged on a broad scale for the visitors' entertainment. Carriages in abundance were in waiting at the depot and the guests were driven rapidly to the elegant Metropole Hotel. Two or three hours were given to the ladies to rest in the sumptuous apartments of that establishment, while their male escorts visited the newspaper offices and took in the sights generally, after which, fortified with a hearty lunch, the carriages were resumed and the procession wound its way through the long, level, unpaved, but smooth, well shaded and watered streets of Denver, and past all the noteworthy buildings, public and private, of that wonderful city, located in 1858 as a

THE HOTEL METROPOLE—DENVER.

mining camp in a desolate prairie region just this side of the shadows of the Rocky Mountains, which loom up about fourteen miles to the Westward. Some of the enormous smelting works on the outskirts of the city were also visited, and an insight was gained of the subtle processes by which rough ores are transmuted into precious metals. Dinner followed, after which the entire party visited the two theatres then in operation in the city, one at the Metropole Hotel and the other the splendid Tabor Grand Opera House, and at the termination of the performances they were transported back to their train, and at 1 A. M. were again speeding Westward, now on the tracks of the Denver and Rio Grande Railroad.

Leaving Denver about 1 A. M., the train three hours later reached Colorado Springs, where, however, it stopped for only a few moments. It had been the expectation of the Pike's Peak Press Club and the Chamber of Commerce that the visitors would be permitted to remain there for a short time to be shown the sights of the locality, but the delay could not be afforded. However, copies of the morning papers were left on the train, and before the breakfast hour was over all the passengers were aware that they had passed through "the Sanitarium City of the West." A similar fact was impressed upon their minds at several other places they visited during the trip.

The ride from Denver was refreshing to exhausted humanity. Sight-seeing was already beginning to pall upon the senses. When the party awoke on the morning of Sunday, January 10th, they found themselves plunging into the very heart of the Rocky Mountains. At seven o'clock they were all routed out from their comfortable berths to inspect the wonderful pathway nature had riven through the rocky barrier that forms the continent's backbone, the Grand Canyon of the Arkansas, better known to tourists as the "Royal Gorge." Here, between majestic walls two thousand feet in height, wonderful engineering skill had contrived a roadway that seemed to be carved for the special purpose through the solid rock. Gazing upwards to the opening in the rift, far overhead, that seemed to touch the heavens, one felt like exclaiming with the Psalmist : "Lift up your heads, O ye gates ; and be ye lifted up, ye everlasting doors ; and the King of glory shall come in." At a point where the Arkansas River is spanned by a bridge suspended by iron braces from the overhanging cliffs on either side, the train was halted, and the passengers were invited to step out into the freezing cold to be photographed by an artist whom Passenger Agent Jerome had enticed for that purpose from Denver. Their pictures being instantly frozen fast to the negative, the party held a brief Service of Song, under the leadership of Mr. Alfred E. Pearsall, of the New York Press Club, "Our Own," as he is familiarly known by his associates in that organization, who, climbing to a giddy height on the rocky wall of the canyon, sang with power and sweetness "America," in which he was joined with vigorous earnestness by the entire party. Probably that was the first Sabbath service ever held in that remote and hardly accessible chasm. Under way again, the train labored up a steep grade, seeking the crest of the Rocky Mountains. It found it, too, for at three in the afternoon

30

Leadville was reached, at an elevation of ten thousand, two hundred feet above the level of the sea, a fact which speedily made itself apparent to lungs with weak pumping power attachments. The visitors having heard much of that famous mining camp were deeply interested in such portion of it as was not hidden from their view by the deep snow. Several of the towns-people being at the depot with sleighs, an impromptu invitation was extended to the visitors to take a short ride, which was participated in with hilarious satisfaction. After leaving Leadville and

GLENWOOD SPRINGS, COLO., WHERE THE PRESS LEAGUE PARTY BATHED IN A SNOW STORM,
JANUARY 10TH, 1892.

surmounting the Rocky Mountains at Tennessee Pass, at an elevation of ten thousand, four hundred and eighteen feet, the train resumed its rapid pace on the down grade, and the run that afternoon through the sublime canyon of the Grand River was a most enjoyable experience. Shortly after dark the train stopped at

THE CANYON OF THE   COLORADO

Glenwood Springs. A blinding snowstorm prevailed, through which the party was conveyed in sleighs about a quarter of a mile to a luxurious hotel, resplendent with electric lights, and furnished in the most approved style of modern artistic decoration. Here was enjoyed one of the most remarkable experiences of the entire journey. The hotel stands on the edge of a pool of steaming hot water supplied from a mineral spring whose temperature is one hundred and twenty degrees, and its outpour two thousand gallons per minute. In the bathing pool at the house the temperature of the water is considerably reduced, and the gentlemen of the party, donning bathing suits, plunged in for a warm out-of-door bath, while the ladies on an upper balcony, protected by umbrellas from the storm, threw snow-balls at the bathers. It really was a very remarkable sight. The night was inky dark, the snow was falling almost in a single sheet, and the electric lights barely penetrated the misty atmosphere to reveal the heads of the men swimming in the steaming pool. Every now and then the snow and cold air combined would induce the bathers to wholly submerge themselves, but their heads would quickly reappear and in a moment would be again incrusted with snow. The proprietor of the establishment and the physician resident there had given full assurances that bathing under those incongruous conditions was entirely harmless. The water was strongly impregnated with salt and sulphur, and open air bathing is practiced there at all times of the day and in all seasons of the year. The participants in the bath, after resuming their traveling attire, found the effect to be rather exhilarating than otherwise, and none of them derived any ill consequence from what would in any other place in the world seem to be a reckless defiance of hygiene and common sense. An hour and a half were most agreeably passed in visiting this remarkable point and

34

exploring, in spite of the darkness and storm, the medicinal springs with which it is surrounded. Returning to the train the berths were sought at an early hour, excepting by a few of the more devoutly inclined, who sat up a while longer singing hymns. Thus was passed the first Sunday of the journey. Glenwood, we learned from our railroad companions, is situated in a "park" two thousand, two hundred feet above the sea-level, protected on every side by lofty mountains, and holding within its limits a series of hot sulphur springs bursting out of the mountain rocks forming lakes of large proportions, and making natural bathing places which by artificial means have been rendered very convenient for the use of man. This hot sulphur water, used as a drink or to bathe in, has been found very efficacious as a remedy in many diseases, and the volume of water is so great that there seems to be no limit to the extent to which it may be utilized, or to the number of people who may partake of or be benefited by it. Above the springs, as they rush out of the rocks, are large open caves which, somewhere within their recesses, must have communication with the hot sulphur water below, as they are filled with hot sulphurous vapor or steam, which rushes out from their mouths in dense clouds. One may enter these caves, divest one's self of clothing, penetrate as far as the heat will allow, and partake of a natural hot sulphur vapor bath such as can be had nowhere else in the world, and which is claimed to be of great remedial or curative value for many complaints that the human frame is afflicted with. The Press League excursionists did not penetrate the mysteries of the locality further than the pools at the hotel. The region is said to be full of game, and the trout fishing superb, so every delegate in the party determined in his mind to wander out that way again, some time, at a more genial season of the year.

35

On Monday morning, January 11th, Salt Lake was reached at eleven o'clock. A delegation of officials, citizens and newspaper men from Salt Lake City met the party at Bingham Junction in a special train, under the charge of J. H. Bennett, General Passenger Agent of the Rio Grande & Western Railroad. Some time previous to the advent of these hospitable gentlemen there had been placed on the train, at a point one hundred and fifty miles east of Salt Lake City, copies of the Salt Lake City *Herald* of that date, and cards of welcome, on which was recited the programme of the entertainment prepared for the passengers during their visit in the City of Saints. On arriving at the depot the visitors were taken in carriages and stages and many in sleighs, as the snow was quite deep and still falling, and were driven to the Knutsford Hotel, where a brief interval was allowed them for resting in some of the three hundred rooms which this fine hotel contains. The party was increased at this point by the addition to its numbers of Mrs. Young, a very lively, Boston-looking young lady, who enjoyed the double honor of being the grand-daughter of Brigham Young, deceased, and the divorced wife of one of that gentleman's sons. After the dust of travel had been removed, the visitors were taken in carriages throughout the city and were shown all the attractions of the place, alighting only to visit the Temple and the Tabernacle.

WHERE WE WERE ENTERTAINED IN
SALT LAKE CITY.

Owing to the incomplete condition of the former, it was not considered safe to enter it on the slippery planks that led

36

SOME OF THE BUILDINGS AND LOCALITIES VISITED AND SEEN IN SALT LAKE CITY.

from the sidewalks. This building is, next to the magnificent St. Patrick's Cathedral in New York, the grandest and most costly ecclesiastical structure in the United States. Begun in 1853, it was said to have cost nearly seven million dollars when, on April 6th, 1892, the last stone was laid, on the thirty-ninth anniversary of the laying of the corner stone. The edifice is two hundred feet long, a hundred feet wide and a hundred feet high, with four towers, one at each corner, two hundred and twenty feet in height. But figures give only an imperfect suggestion of its great size. The walls are ten feet thick, and the massiveness and solidity of its construction insure its defiance of the ravages of time for ages to come. It is built wholly of snow-white granite, and, standing on one of the loftiest points in the city, it can be seen for many miles up and down the valley. The Temple is not intended to be a house of worship, but will be used wholly for conducting the ceremonial rites of the Mormon priesthood. The Tabernacle in the same square is one of the architectural curiosities of the world. It looks like a vast terrapin-back or half of a prodigious egg-shell cut in two lengthwise, and is built wholly of glass, iron and stone. It is two hundred and fifty feet long, a hundred and fifty feet wide and a hundred feet high in the center of the roof, which is a single mighty arch, unsupported by pillar or post, and is said to have but one counterpart on the globe. The walls are twelve feet thick, and there are twenty huge double doors for entrance and exit. In the same enclosure is still another spacious structure, in which, we were informed, were held the regular church services of the Mormons. It is called Assembly Hall, is of white granite, of Gothic architecture and has seats for twenty-five hundred. The ceiling is elaborately frescoed with scenes from Mormon history, including the delivery of the golden plates, containing the New Revelation, to the Prophet Joseph Smith by the Angel Moroni. The Hall contains a superb organ of native woods and home workmanship. The visitors received these facts on faith, as they did not enter the Hall. But the peculiar architectural features of the Tabernacle were thoroughly exploited, including the verification of that enormous structure's acoustic properties. The seating capacity of the building is said to be fourteen thousand. The visitors being stationed at the end furthest from the raised platform where the vast organ stands, one of the

ASSEMBLY HALL, THE TABERNACLE AND THE NEW MORMON TEMPLE IN SALT LAKE CITY.

local committee, enjoining silence, dropped a common pin from his hand on a board where he was standing. The sound of that tiny piece of metal striking the board was distinctly heard by every person at the distant end of the apartment. Similar experiments were made by whispering across the room, the voice being in like manner as distinctly audible as is the case in the world renowned Whispering Gallery of St. Paul's Church in London. Leaving that interesting place, the guests were driven past the Tithing

House, the Beehive House and the Lion House, half hidden by the high surrounding wall, the residence of the late Brigham Young, and the residences of eighteen of his numerous wives; experience evidently having shown him that domestic felicity, when essayed in such off-hand fashion, could only be approximately achieved by keeping his spouses in separate residences. The ladies of the party manifested a decided interest in the evidences of the peculiar institution which has given Mormondom its notoriety, but they were wise enough to use great discretion in the inquiries they made of the gentlemen who acted as escorts on the occasion. On one point the entire party were unanimously agreed, and that was in admiration of the beauty of Salt Lake City, its wide streets and its picturesque location in the mountain-framed valley. The season of the year, however, was not propitious to seeing Salt Lake City at its greatest advantage, and the guests were repeatedly invited to come again later in the year, when, it was said, the whole city would bear the appearance of a luxuriant flower garden. The place is rapidly being transferred into Gentile hands, from those of the Mormons, who founded it under Brigham Young in the summer of 1847. As is fitting to a city built in a vast wilderness, it was laid out on a scale of majestic proportions, the streets being one hundred and thirty-two feet in width and the blocks comprising each ten square acres, the distance from street to street being everywhere just six hundred and sixty-six and two-thirds feet. On each side of every thoroughfare is a wide ditch of running water from the mountains- the irrigating system, that at great cost of labor and money converted the arid waste on which the Saints planted their settlement into a latter day Paradise. Every house seems to be surrounded by a lawn and garden or orchard. But if the beauty of the city, its possibility, in fact, was due to Mormon perseverance in the past, its present development is wholly owing to the spirit of modern progress which has actuated it under Gentile control within the last decade. Since 1880 the population has increased from twenty-one thousand to nearly fifty-five thousand persons, whose wealth per capita is said to be greater than that of any other community in the United States. Think of a town on the backbone of the continent possessing sixty-five miles of electric street railways!

Returning to the hospitable Knutsford Hotel, a fine lunch was partaken of, after which the visitors passed the time in looking around on their own account. The newspaper offices, the *Tribune* and the *Herald*, were visited in force. Many of the ladies repaired to their apartments to rest. Quite a number of the travelers, however, accepted an invitation from the Union Pacific Railroad to make a trip in a special train to Garfield Beach to get a near-by view of Salt Lake. Later in the day an excursion was also made to the recently discovered natural gas wells some miles out of the city. It was so late in the day that it was dark when the wells were reached. The spectacle, however, was the more brilliant on that account, the Gas Company having run out a line of pipe from one of the wells, so that there were flambeaux at various points along the path leading from the cars, the flames in some cases reaching to a height of fully fifty feet. The Pittsburgh visitors had an opportunity at this point of displaying their familiarity with natural gas, and had there been any Chicago representatives in the party, they, too, might have enjoyed a similar privilege. It was 7.45 P. M. when the excursion train of six cars returned to the city, and the passengers made a bee line from the depot to the Tabernacle, where a grand concert had been announced to be given for their special benefit. The Choral Society of Salt Lake City and the choir of the Tabernacle, numbering jointly five hundred voices, officiated under the direction of Conductor Stephens. Prof. Radcliffe performed on the magnificent organ, said to have cost $100,000 and to be the second largest in the world. It is fifty-eight feet high and contains two thousand six hundred and forty-eight pipes. A delightful programme was performed by the monster combination of local talent, and the visitors likewise took a hand in the entertainment by pressing Mr. Pearsall into giving one of his excellent recitations, which was followed by Marshall P. Wilder, who amused the audience with a series of droll anecdotes. This circumstance is the more significant from the fact that it was the first time that the Tabernacle had been lent to such purely secular uses as those represented by the two gentlemen from New York, and it was understood afterward that we had just anticipated the date when, by an edict of the rulers of the church, the edifice could never again be similarly used.

Messrs. Wilder and Pearsall were accordingly congratulated upon being personally concerned in an epoch in the ecclesiastical history of Mormondom. The whole affair was exceedingly enjoyable, outside of its qualified historic significance. Returning to the hotel, after an agreeable collation, a brilliant reception was given to the visitors, which was participated in by most of the prominent citizens Gentile and Mormon of the place. The guests were gathered in a spacious dining hall of the hotel, and Judge O. W. Powers, of Illinois, who occupied the chair for the evening, delivered a charming welcoming address. He was followed by Gov. Thomas, after whom followed brief and telling addresses by the President of the League, Mr. T. J. Keenan; Judge Goodwin, in behalf of the " Rocky Mountain Press"; Kate Field, in behalf of " Woman as a Business Man"; the Hon. George Q. Cannon, the distinguished Mormon leader, who, as a pioneer printer, spoke for the "Hand-Cart Brigade"; Mr. Keeler, of Boston, in response to the toast, "The Salt Lake of the East"; the Hon. W. H. King, for "One of Utah's Best Crops"; Ex-Gov. West, as speeding the departing guests; Mr. Coates, of New York, on behalf of Press Clubs generally, and Fred. Simon, on behalf of Utah in the con-

MISS KATE FIELD, OF WASHINGTON, D. C.

crete and abstract. In addition to the speeches of the evening, some charming vocalism was rendered by Miss Lillie Snyder; Mrs. Frank Leslie repeated a stirring poem on the onward progress of "Columbus";

MRS. FRANK LESLIE.

a recitation was given by Miss Elita Proctor Otis, of New York, and a series of laughable stories were told by Marshall P. Wilder, who, with the recollection still strong on him of his performance at the Temple, was in cheerful vein, and was repeatedly recalled to the front. The evening passed quickly in that delightful manner, and it was one o'clock in the morning when the party again found themselves on their train, speeding yet further westward towards the Pacific.

Brief glimpses were obtained at intervals of the Great Salt Lake as the train swept along its southern shore, and at 3 A. M. on January 12th our hospitable hosts of the Rio Grande & Western Railroad were bidden a reluctant farewell as we were switched on to the Southern Pacific Railroad, in whose charge we were to remain for the following twelve days. The entire day was passed in overcoming the Sierra Nevadas, and when evening arrived and we were being whirled through the canyons and the snow-sheds of that majestic range of mountains, the whole party were assembled in the dining car to listen to the reading of a "newspaper," the several contributions to which were prepared during the day by some of the more enterprising of the delegates, under the editorial supervision of Mr. Foster Coates. It was the first evening paper ever brought out in that section of the continent, and probably nowhere else on the continent has a new journalistic enterprise ever made such rapid headway. The next morning found us in Auburn, California.

CHAPTER II.

CONVENTION DAYS.

JANUARY 13-20, 1892.

AT AUBURN we were suddenly introduced to California, and to say that our introduction was a revelation to the entire party would be far from exaggeration. Placer County, in which we now were, is called the "Gateway" to the Golden State. With the snowdrifts in full view around us and the Arctic cold of the Sierra Nevadas still fresh in our memories, we seemed, on that warm, sunshiny morning, to have passed through the gateway that leads directly from perpetual winter to everlasting summer. Here, indeed, was the complete realization of the poet's ideal Auburn,

"Where smiling spring its earliest visit paid,
And parting summer's lingering blooms delayed."

The train passing through an immense arch of oranges and flowers drew up at a depot resplendent with floral decorations. Among a variety of devices the word "Welcome" greeted us above the platform, framed with golden oranges. The decorative possibilities of the orange were visible at nearly every house in the place. A committee of citizens was on hand with carriages, and the party was conveyed to two hotels, the Putnam and the Freeman House, where excellent breakfasts were discussed, which, as we had arisen from our Wagner couches at an unusually early hour, were particularly welcome. The champagne cocktails of native vintage

45

that were set before us as a preliminary to the meal might, under such circumstances, have prompted a responsive thrill in the heart of the most unmitigated apostle of Prohibition. But the magnificent flowers and the decorations of fruit with which the tables and apartments overflowed, were, next to the charming ladies who gave the grace of their presence to welcome us to

California, the most striking features of that brilliant and memorable morning. Breakfast finished, and two or three short greetings having been interchanged by the orators on both sides, to carriage again, to visit the Citrus Fair in "The Pavilion," a newly erected theatre, where the reality of that land of sun and flowers, in which the fruit harvest reaches from January to December, was dis-

SACRAMENTO'S ORANGE ARCH AT AUBURN, CAL.

played in a manner none of the visitors had ever dreamed of. Besides apples, pears and plums, in great abundance and variety, oranges, lemons, grapes, figs, dates, olives, almonds and other tropical fruits and products were massed about the building in tasteful shapes and in vast quantities, the growth of that section of Northern California comprising ten counties which a few years ago were hardly known of as agriculturally capable. Thirty-six varieties of oranges, and six of lemons, all large, highly colored and well rounded fruit, constituted two only of the host of displays on exhibition there, that gladdened all the senses. Among the varied devices, a conspicuous one was a monster horn of plenty, made entirely of oranges, and pouring from its capacious mouth a stream of luscious fruits, the exhibit of Sutter County.

CORNUCOPIA OF ORANGES—SUTTER COUNTY'S EXHIBIT AT THE AUBURN CITRUS FAIR.

At Auburn, also, we discovered that we had reached the longitude of comparative magnitudes, a geographical peculiarity which we were not suffered to lose sight of while we remained on the Pacific slope. The precise relation of Placer County, California, in respect to size, to the State of Massachusetts, or to the whole of the eastern States, or to the rest of the earth, has escaped the writer's memory, but the proportion calculator had got us into his clutches, and we speedily learned to regard his fertility of

47

imagination and ingenuity of combination with unspeakable awe.
From the Pavilion we were driven to a point near the town
named Aeolia Heights, where among trees and vineyards, on a
commanding eminence, Col. W. Hamilton, of Sacramento, has a
charming lodge fitted with exquisite taste, and overlooking a vast
wooded gorge, at the bottom of which runs the American River.
It was a landscape of unsurpassed loveliness.   But we had not
yet reached our destination, so at 10.30 A. M., after brief speech-
making and cordial hand-shaking, we resumed our journey.
Every member of the party will carry enduring recollection of
the reluctance with which we parted from the sweet, half-tropical
vision that had been presented to our eyes that morning on our
entrance into California.

On reaching Auburn our train was increased by the addition
of two remarkably well stocked cars containing a delegation
headed by Mr. M. H. de Young, and comprising President Hugh
Hume, Gen. John F. Sheehan and Gen. John S. McComb, with
a large party of lively volunteers, sent to welcome us on behalf of
the San Francisco Press Club.   From that moment until we left
San Francisco, one week afterward, we were in the hands of that
Club as its guests, and never in newspaper history was royal
hospitality more lavishly or more gracefully bestowed.   The
correctness of this statement will develop as we proceed.   Stopping
for an hour at Sacramento, we were greeted with a fresh
surprise, the San Francisco newspapers of that date, particularly
the *Examiner* and the *Chronicle*, having prepared a welcome for
us in the shape of special dispatches containing the latest news
from the home of almost every member of the party.   We
arrived in San Francisco about four in the afternoon, and soon
were snugly ensconced in the Baldwin Hotel, where rooms had
been bespoken for and assigned to us in advance.

SOME OF THE WOMEN DELEGATES AND GUESTS

Mrs. F. E. Owens,   Mrs. J. Merrill,
Mrs. Elroy Avery,   Miss Belle L. Gordon,
   Mrs. Lucy Corral,   Mrs. J. P. Dandman,   Mrs. Mary A. West,
          Miss Boyer,   Mrs. P. C. Baker.

We had reached the Pacific Coast. At this stage of the narrative the pen involuntarily pauses as memory recalls the succession of incidents upon whose description it is about to enter. The series of brilliant entertainments, such as were never before showered upon a party of amazed visitors; the beautiful scenery which they were invited to enjoy, the wonders of nature they were confronted with, the steady jump at which they were kept moving, the palatial residences at which they were welcomed, and, above and beyond all else, the magnificent friendliness with which they were greeted, collectively and individually, by their big-hearted Californian hosts, would require a volume to adequately relate, and would tax the powers of an abler writer than the present one to competently describe. To each member of the party who reads these pages there will doubtless recur many facts and incidents that dwell fondly in his memory as among the most enjoyable of his experiences on the trip, but of which he will find here no record. In some respects a narrative like this is like men's lives, the checkered fabric of whose careers is made up of threads of personal encounter, which cross and recross each other in the weaving, but always preserve their separate identity. It is the nearness together of the points of contact that imparts the character to the texture. So this short story of travel must necessarily be traced along the line of the writer's personal observation of incidents in which all participated, but with differing points of joint experience.

The first night in San Francisco was variously employed by the visiting party. The officers of the League and a few specially invited persons were entertained at a dinner party by Mr. M. H. de Young, proprietor of the San Francisco *Chronicle*, upon whom had centered the unanimous determination of the Eastern Press Club men and women as their selection for the next

President of the League. That they were splendidly entertained needs no emphasis. Mr. de Young's residence is one of the many private palaces for which San Francisco is famous, and as the guests crossed the threshold they beheld a scene that each will long remember. The wide hall was hung with tapestries and adorned with marble statuettes on richly ornate pedestals, and with decorated vases holding palms and fragrant flowers, all glowing in the soft light shed by a myriad of gas jets gleaming through tinted shades. Over the doorway leading to the banquet room hung a white satin banner bearing in golden letters, these words of greeting: "With mystic key, our glorious State, unlocks for thee the Golden Gate." On the right of the arch was a branch of a giant redwood, and on the other side an orange bough laden with golden fruit, their junction over the arch being adorned with chrysanthemums intermixed with ferns and tendrils of green bamboo. The dining-room was decorated with similar elegance, and at each guest's plate lay a card of unique design, bearing his name in golden letters. The soft strains of a string band, hidden in some fern-curtained corner, made a mellifluous accompaniment to the clattering of knife and fork and glass as the party discussed the exquisite menu and offered their libations in wines of rarest vintage. At the close of the repast, Marshall P. Wilder set the fun in motion with some droll narratives, which were succeeded by brief and telling

THE "CHRONICLE" OFFICE, SAN FRANCISCO.

addresses by Mr. de Young, Mr. Hume, President of the San
Francisco Press Club; Messrs. Berri, Page and Coates, of New
York; Mayor Sanderson, Gen. Ruger, U. S. A., and Mr. Hazelton,
editor of the San Francisco *Post*. Then the guests were led to
the unique apartment in the basement of Mr. de Young's house,
known as the Chinese Room, where they were served with coffee
and cigars. That room was one of the wonders of the trip. On
every side were displayed rare specimens of cunning carving, while
chairs and tables of costly wood and quaint design stood around in
cozy attractiveness. The walls were embellished with Chinese masks
and weapons, and on one side was a hideous idol, surmounted
with a dragon, before which, doubtless, many generations of wor-
shippers in China have bent their knees in adoration. The hangings
of this strangely brilliant saloon, the mouldings and all the
decorations and ornaments, were from the Celestial Kingdom, and
their effect upon the visitors was weirdly impressive. There is no
other similarly adorned apartment in any residence in the United
States. The party broke up at a late hour and returned to the
hotel, conversing in a strange patois of mixed Chinese and Heidsieck.
The young men of the delegation were regaled that same evening
at a "Late Watch" at the Press Club, where "high jinks" and
"low jinks," and assorted provocatives of hilarity, were enjoyed
until the early watches of the next day had begun. The convivial
chairman of the Entertainment Committee, Mr. Gagan, with his
ever courteous associates, Messrs. Lawrence, Denny and Barendt,
and the omnipresent Hume, who had stolen away from the de
Young banquet to join in welcoming the visitors, were indefatigable in their fun-inspiring efforts, and even the bashful New
York delegates were speedily thawed out from the icy reserve in
which they are customarily enveloped. Mr. Williams, of the Club,
tendered to the League the freedom of the city, which Mayor

Sanderson afterward confirmed, with the further pledge that the police regulations would be suspended in San Francisco on their behalf throughout the Convention. It was possibly owing to this judicious municipal prevision that the League was enabled as an entire body to participate in the festivities of the following week. Mr. Bromley made an amusing speech, in the course of which he conferred upon the guests whatever portion of the city remained unbestowed; and with songs, recitations and a variety of admirable musical performances, that memorable "Late Watch" was a very lively initiation into the ways of San Francisco journalists.

Meanwhile, with greater prudence, the rest of the party had succumbed to the attractions of their luxurious apartments in "The Baldwin," and had retired betimes to enjoy the first night's repose in bed they had experienced since leaving home. These probably were the wisest of all, for no future opportunity for genuine all night rest was afforded during the entire journey.

That there should be no doubt as to the hospitable intentions of their hosts, each of the visitors received at his apartment an elegant, vellum-bound Souvenir book, illustrated and exquisitely printed on heavy cream-laid paper, in which the San Francisco Press Club outlined the programme for the coming week. This programme, which was accurately adhered to, was introduced by the following words of welcome :

Welcome, oh, delegates from the frozen East, from the crank-crowded purlieus of New York, from the city of the Lake, where no man dare wear whiskers, from the fever-haunted swamps of Indiana, from the blizzard-swept plains of Dakota, from the arid deserts of Utah, where the thermometer ranges from forty-two below to one hundred and forty above in the shade, from the cattle trails of Nebraska, from the pork-laden plains of Ohio, from the sage-brush of Nevada, where the voice of the jack-rabbit is heard in the land and the coyote is the king of beasts-- welcome, thrice welcome, to California!!!

53

Welcome, oh, welcome, men of the East, North and South, and ten times welcome, ladies from the lands on the thither side of the Sierra Nevadas! Welcome to California, where the noise of the flowers growing in January is like unto the roar of an avalanche, and strawberries are in season all the year round; where the climate is sold by the acre and land by the quart; and where you can wear a linen duster in winter and a blanket in summer—if you wish to.

We are here to bid you welcome. Come into the hacienda and partake of frijoles; tie your horses to the corn bin and let them eat; throw your guns and knives into the corner, for you are among friends. All that we have is yours; would that we had more.

Welcome, a hundred times welcome, oh, ladies from the lands where the violet does not bloom until the end of spring, and the only orange blossoms to be found are on the heads of the brides! All California bids you welcome. The tall redwoods of the forest will bow to the ground as you pass by, the grizzly bears and the lions will sing serenades beneath your windows, and the rivers will leave their beds at a moment's notice to make things pleasant for you. Welcome, a thousand welcomes, oh, delegates and friends! The whole Pacific coast is waiting to do you honor. The salmon has left his home in the mighty Columbia to sit with you at the feast; and his young companion, the shrimp, will be at his side. The juicy canvas-back, lovely of plumage and mighty of pinion, will contribute to your happiness; and the effusion of the grape from a hundred sun-kissed Californian hillsides shall flow in your honor.

The country is all yours. From the snow-capped Shasta in the North to the tropic verges of Los Angeles and Santa Barbara; from the lava beds of Modoc to the burning sands of Arizona; from Mount Whitney to Mount Diablo; in short, "from the Siskiyou to San Diego, from the Sierras to the sea," you shall roam where you please, take what you please, and do what you please. For this occasion the San Francisco Press Club owns the earth and places it at your feet.

Would you bathe in the warm waters of Del Monte; speed behind the fastest horses of Palo Alto; drink dry the breweries or drain the mighty vat of Vina--do so; they are all at your service. The loveliest ladies of our land shall smile on your braves, and the bravest men kneel at the feet of your fair ones. The land is yours, and, in the language of the postmaster's poet, "if you don't see what you want, please ask for it."

The roses are growing in the vales for you, and the early asparagus has pushed his head through the earth to peep at the procession. We have warm hearts and cold bottles at your service. You have come out of the wilderness into the Garden of Eden, and there is no reservation on the apples. The breeze will blow from the West while you are with us, and if you smile, our generous earth will crack its sides till you think you have met a Californian Earthquake.

California is nine hundred miles long and from one hundred and thirty-eight to one hundred and forty miles wide, and embodies all that is best of the entire globe in that compass. Sample the goods that the gods have given us; reform, and become a Californian. All the zones are here—torrid, frigid and temperate within a half day's journey of each other, and ozone in every one of them; so that fondness for previous conditions of existence can form no excuse.

Welcome, again!

The visitors were also presented with handsome silver buttons, artistic symbols of close attachment, having engraved on one side the sun setting in the Pacific and on the reverse the words "International League of Press Clubs, San Francisco." From that time forward the Eastern guests when they fancied a want was unsatisfied, had only to press the button—the San Francisco Press Club "did the rest."

Thursday, January 14th, was a bright, sunshiny day, with a warmth suggestive of the latter part of May in New York. It had been the intention to hold a session of the Convention in the forenoon, but that plan was unanimously and perhaps somewhat vociferously abandoned when the local committee announced that carriages were in waiting to take the excursionists to Sutro Heights, to view the famous Golden Gate. The fact began to dawn upon our excited minds that we had traveled four thousand miles on false pretenses. While we had been pretending all the way across the continent that we were going to California purely on Press Club business of weighty moment, we really were bent on sight-seeing and enjoyment. It is only fair to state that this view of the case was not entertained, even secretly, by any one of the Eastern visitors, until it was forced upon their consciences by their San Francisco hosts. Nevertheless, much Convention business was transacted before we left San Francisco—but it was no fault of our entertainers that we were allowed to attend to it. Surreptitious advantage was taken of their unguarded moments—of very infrequent occurrence—when a slight lull happened in the torrent of entertainment, to sneak in an hour or so, and once even a whole forenoon, of real work. (It seems now, on deliberate reflection, to have been rather unfair conduct on our part towards

those who treated us throughout with such frank open-handedness.) This parenthesis is necessary to explain how we happened to go to Sutro Park that morning, instead of following the programme announced by the Governing Board before we left New York. It is no spirit of vanity that impels the assertion that we presented a splendid appearance as we rode through and around San Francisco that morning, for it is only a surmise on the writer's part, based upon the attention the procession everywhere attracted. Some were in coaches, some in commodious stages and some contented themselves on the top of a tally-ho, whose four spirited horses were "tooled" by no less a personage than our host, "Lucky Baldwin," to whom the turnout belonged. After climbing some of the seven hills on which San Francisco, like Rome, is founded, we were driven through the beautiful Golden Gate Park, where our hosts informed us "there are no keep-off-the-grass signs, and where the whole population has room to breathe. In June or December,

GOLDEN GATE FROM THE TERRACE AT
SUTRO HEIGHTS.

winter or summer, there are acres of flowers and all out of doors. The deer have a valley to themselves, the buffalo have a whole hillside. One part of the Park is for the children alone. There are hills and meadows, thick woods and beautiful lawns, miles of glorious drives and shady walks. The Park extends to the ocean beach, where the billows of the great Pacific ceaselessly break and roar." All this we verified, and enjoyed immensely. An hour was spent inspecting the manifold beauties of the Conservatory, where a day would have been too short a time for making a perfect examination, and, finally, down a steep hill and up a steeper one, and we entered the beautiful grounds belonging to Adolph Sutro, of Nevada silver mining and Comstock tunnel fame. Just before arriving, we were met by Mr. Sutro himself, mounted on a spirited

thoroughbred, which he rode with dignified grace, who escorted us around the winding roads, amid groves and flower beds and statuary, to the Cliff House. There we found ourselves face to face with the Golden Gate, with the Pacific Ocean spreading its vast expanse before us, shimmering almost without a ripple

SEAL ROCKS SEEN FROM SUTRO HEIGHTS.

in the brilliant sunshine. Near at hand were the famous Seal Rocks, covered with hundreds of those curious phocids, with the bland

countenances of statesmen and the slippery habits of politicians, sunning themselves in affectionate groups as they barked their welcome to the visitors. A detailed inspection was made of the princely domain, which Mr. Sutro has transformed from a sand-hill into a Golden State Eden by the exercise of the same Californian magic as that with which he had raised himself from poverty to conspicuous wealth, after which lunch was served on

LUNCHEON ON THE PORCH OF THE SUTRO RESIDENCE, JANUARY 14TH, 1892.

the porch of the Sutro residence, where two long tables were laid, whose only shelter was an awning for protection from the sun. This exquisite repast, partaken of amid ripening fruits and blooming flowers on the shore of the Pacific Ocean in the open air in January, was the forerunner of many contrasts with home experiences which the visitors were about to have brought to their attention. No subsequent occasion on the entire journey weakened the deep impression of that elegant entertainment or in any degree conflicted with the agreeable remembrances that were imparted by the brilliant spectacle of a winter out-door festivity, where all the attributes of wealth, hospitality, beauty, intellect and nature's most charming aspects were so skilfully and so harmoniously blended.

Fully two hours were occupied in discussing the lunch, the menu being contrived of dishes peculiar to the California region, seasoned with wines and fruits of native growth. A few short speeches succeeded the repast, Mr. Sutro leading in words of cordial greeting, followed by Messrs. Berri, Welshons and Page. At three o'clock the party broke up and the visitors were driven back to San Francisco, past the Golden Gate and through the entire breadth of the beautiful military reservation of the Presidio. Late in the afternoon the opening session of the Convention was held in the Press Club rooms in Pine Street, and in the evening a brilliant reception was held at the same place, which was graced by the presence of the leading representatives of San Francisco's social worth and feminine beauty. The handsome club rooms were charmingly arrayed for the occasion, the walls being hung with paintings and decorated with tasteful adornments. Vases of palms and ferns were artistically disposed, the deep green of their spreading leaves making a reposeful background to the brilliant kaleidoscopic effects of color that gleamed and fluttered on the floors in constantly changing combinations.

MR. SUTRO'S AQUARIUM AND BATHS AT THE CLIFF HOUSE.

The effect was in every way charming to the senses. During the evening an excellent musical programme by several prominent artists was rendered. The visitors in whose honor the entertainment was given were overwhelmed with attentions, their hosts leaving nothing undone that graceful hospitality, coupled with considerate forethought and controlled by cultured taste, could devise for their gratification. It was on this evening that the Eastern party arrived at the unanimous conclusion, which was reiterated daily during their stay in California, that the immediate occasion, whenever and wherever it occurred, was the most delightful experience of the whole journey. When enjoyment is thus steadily and progressively augmented, how inadequately weak words are to give it proportionate expression. It is, of course, impracticable within the scope of the present narrative to enter into minute details of what was done and who did it, or what was said and who said it, or what was seen and who provided it, at all the enjoyable gatherings which greeted the travelers along their route. Something must be left to the reader's imagination, and even that flexible faculty may be vigorously strained and yet not stretch to the full gauge of the subject. The San Francisco Press Club reception, however, possessed a special interest, as, excepting the committee who had received us at Auburn, it was the first time that we had been brought collectively into personal communication with the gentlemen of whose hospitalities we were partaking. To the visitors, at least, the relationship thus set on foot was most agreeable. The entertainment had an additional attractiveness in the introduction it afforded us to a brilliant element of San Francisco society. The bar, the bench, the pulpit and the army were all conspicuously represented, besides the leading lights of the city's literary and artistic circles, and as to the ladies there present, suffice it to say that they were in every respect charming and attractive. Press Club entertainments of that order are not often witnessed in any city.

The morning of Friday, January 15th, was ushered in by rosy-fingered Aurora with the brilliancy of its predecessor for the special delectation of the Eastern visitors. The Pacific newspaper men must have made some special arrangement with the weather bureau, for although according to the almanac the rainy season was at its height, the rains ceased to fall on the day before the Wagner train arrived at Auburn, and sunshine prevailed constantly while the party remained in California. This second day was spent on the water, visiting by special steamer, the "Relief," the points of interest that skirt the beautiful Bay of San Francisco. A number of ladies and gentlemen from the city accompanied the party, and a fine brass band lent its melody to the every way delightful trip. The Union Iron Works, on Mare Island, where, under the conduct

THE GOLDEN GATE AT FORT POINT.

of Mr. Irving M. Scott, several Government war vessels, including the "Monterey" and the "California," were in process of construction, were thoroughly inspected, and the excursionists were then taken around Fort Point and through the Golden Gate to the Seal Rocks, which they had viewed on the previous day from the beautiful terraces of the Sutro domain. The progress of the tug through the harbor was greeted by the dipping of flags and firing of guns by the vessels it passed. Thence the boat steamed to lovely Sausalito, where the voyagers were regaled with a sparkling luncheon at the quarters of the Pacific Yacht Club. This repast, apart from its own intrinsic merits, was noteworthy as being the one and only one public meal partaken of by the travelers during the month of January, 1892, at which no speeches were permitted. The orators of the party bore their deprivation with reasonably good grace.

and the listening element did not seem to have their appetites seriously affected by the omission. About three o'clock the return trip began and the steamer visited San Pablo Bay and passed through Roccoon Straits, heading about for home on arriving at Red Rock. It was five o'clock when the lines were made fast to the Clay street pier. Some of the party hastened to the Palace Hotel, where a reception was being given to the Eastern ladies under the auspices of the Pacific Women's Press Club. The guests were cordially received and most handsomely entertained in exquisitely decorated apartments by a committee of ladies, conspicuous among whom were Mrs. de Young, Mrs. Hugh Hume, Mrs. Townsend, Mrs. Frona E. Wait, Mrs. Christien and Mrs. Black. By the delegates the remainder of the day until late dinner time was devoted to the affairs of the Convention. As this narrative, however, relates exclusively to the business activities that marked the journey, no note is taken of the occasional hours of relaxation enjoyed in Convention diversions. Those agreeable episodes are duly recorded in Secretary Price's Report, where, also, are described, with official elegance, various fascinating accompaniments of the Convention, including the first half of the "Open Session" that was held that evening at the Powell Street Opera House, the unrecorded second part being a midnight inspection of "Chinatown" by the visitors, who explored that unsavory celestial colony in the heart of San Francisco in several detachments, each under the guidance of a detective officer. It is not essential to go into detail regarding what was seen and smelled that night. The list would comprise highbinders, joss houses, fruit venders, theatres, tea stores, opium joints, lodging houses and subterranean dives, ranging in elegance from the pretentious temples, with their gilded and carved ornaments, to the underground places of abode whose chief advertisement was an all-pervading, insinuating, soul-crushing

A GROUP OF DELEGATES FROM EAST AND WEST

M. P. M[...]   JULIUS M[...]
              P. C. [...]
DR. FRIEDERICH,   J. P. DAMEEN
      JULIUS S[...]   T. HENRY MARTIN.

and utterly indescribable stench. If the two and seventy several and well-defined stenches which Coleridge analyzed in the city of Cologne could be combined and concentrated into one vaporous fusion, the result would be a savory suggestion of Araby the Blest in comparison with the fetid effluvium in which the home life of San Francisco Chinatown is perpetually immersed. With the understanding imparted by the guides that there were yet lower degrees of filthiness in the Chinese section than had been exhibited, the satiated visitors, with unanimous impulse, determined to return to the hotel. The record of that evening would be incomplete without mention of the entertainment given by the German Press Club to the Fatherland's contingent of the League delegation. The affair was informal and jolly—"*Ganz famos,*" as one of the party declared the next day. Speeches were made, songs were sung, reminiscences were exchanged, and beer—and that only—was drunk, and the hour hand was reaching out vigorously toward the time for another day to dawn when, with cordial "*Ade: Auf Wiedersehen,*" and earnest handshakes, the party broke up.

On Saturday, January 16th, everybody was routed out at an uncomfortably early hour, considering that none had retired until long after one in the morning. But our hosts were inexorable. Indications were beginning to manifest themselves on the part of the visitors of a disposition to settle permanently in San Francisco, and it was indispensable that they should be removed from the place before the complaint became chronic. Accordingly, at eight o'clock a special train furnished by the Southern Pacific Railroad Company steamed out from San Francisco with two hundred passengers on board, bound for a three days' excursion to Monterey, Santa Cruz and San Jose. The writer of these pages was especially gratified by the companionship on this excursion of an esteemed friend, Mr. Arpad Haraszthy, the well known viticulturist, whose extensive wine cellars are prominent objects of interest in San Francisco, and to whom he was indebted for repeated courtesies during his stay in that city. It was a charming day as the train rattled along the shore of the beautiful Bay and afterward through the fertile Santa Clara Valley, whose abundant vegetation, already far progressed towards ripening, made the frozen fields of the East, so lately traversed, seem immeasurably distant. The first stop was at Menlo Park and the Palo Alto stock farm of Senator Leland Stanford, where the party disembarked and were shown the equine treasures of the farm, including the famous stallion, Palo Alto, the champion trotter of the world, of fabulous value, but fated to die from pneumonia a few months later. After visiting the training track and witnessing how the young animals are broken to their gait, carriages were taken to the Leland Stanford, Jr., University, the grandest monument to paternal affection in existence, and destined to become one of the leading educational institutions in the world. President Jordan received the party with a hearty welcome and escorted them through the grounds and buildings. This institution was founded by Senator Stanford, of California, in memory of his only son, Leland Stanford, Jr., who died a few years ago while pursuing his education abroad. The total present endowment is estimated at $20,000,000, which includes twenty thousand acres of the land surrounding it. The preliminary buildings had recently been completed at the time of our visit and the university opened with over four hundred students on its rolls. The set of buildings which we saw in use are in the form of a large quadrangle, surrounded by one-story structures of dove-colored stone, which, on the inner side facing the quadrangle have cloistered porches, extending all around and broken by handsome

65

arches that serve for entrances to the inner court. The buildings
already erected form the nucleus for a city of schools which it is
expected will extend for several miles. Already there were in

"TOMMY" EVANS, THE YOUNGEST DELEGATE IN THE PARTY.

them a large number of regular departments of the university,
laboratories, lecture rooms, libraries, workshops, etc., in full
operation.

Again we were speeding in the cars past farms and vineyards,

ARIZONA GARDEN.

GLIMPSE OF DEL MONTE.

HOTEL DEL MONTE.

FLOWER PLOTS, DEL MONTE.

Johnson.
Photo.

FROM THE EAST VERANDAH, DEL MONTE.

THE HOTEL DEL MONTE AND ITS GROUNDS.

through the smiling Santa Clara Valley, until at one o'clock
the train arrived at Monterey, and, after passing through a
handsome park-like grove, the magnificent Hotel Del Monte, encom-
passed by one hundred and thirty acres of forest and garden,
opened its hospitable doors, and the realm of fairyland was
entered. Here, in mid-January, in a wilderness of flowers and
verdure, surrounded by a vast wooded park, in which are embodied
all the exquisite possibilities of skillful landscape gardening, near
the shores of a bay as blue as that of Naples, stood a palace, a
masterwork of artistic taste, the culmination of refinement and
luxury. The whole scene was like a realization of a delightful
vision of the imagination. The soft, reposeful charm of Monterey
Bay has received expression in the following lines published in
the *California Magazine :*

> On sea-washed rocks a dainty lichen grows ;
> > Back from the shore are lofty cypress trees ;
> > And in the waves the frail anemones
> Softly their purple fringes ope and close.
> A lonely gull on slow wing seaward goes :
> > A shallop drifts before the freshening breeze ;
> > Full are the lingering hours of calm and ease ;
> Full is the soul, world-weary, of repose.
>
> The wind is singing to the monotone
> > Of the deep tides ; and singing in the pines,
> > Through whose soft waving foliage lightly shines
> The sun on silver beaches as it shone
> > Twelve decades past, when from the branches swung
> > The Mission bells that Junipero hung.

Monterey is one of the quaintest and most interesting places
in California. Located by its Spanish discoverer, Vizcalno, in
1602, it was here that nearly two centuries later the old Mission

Fathers first established themselves, and their little cluster of adobe
houses, and the churches in which they ministered to their savage
flocks, still stand on the shore of the bay, facing the Pacific
Ocean, dreamy reminders of the days of Junipero Serra, when
the king of Spain yet claimed that region as part of his domain.
A granite statue marks the spot where Padre Junipero landed in
1770, and not far distant, in strange historic contrast, are the ruins
of Fremont's Fort, where, in 1847, the "Pathfinder" first raised
the bear-emblazoned flag, when the golden State was wrested
from Mexico. The experiences of that afternoon will never be
forgotten. The delightful ride of eighteen miles to wave-dashed
Cypress Point, along broad, smooth avenues, now skirting the
very water's edge, now passing through dense pine and live oak
forests, or traversing the California Chautauqua, Pacific Grove,
or through quaint settlements of Chinese fishermen, then bringing
up by the sea shore at an abrupt point, beyond which are ledges
of rocks covered with seals, is, beyond any question, one of the
grandest drives in the world. At one point it passes through
a grove of singular trees, found only in one other place on earth.
They are cedars of Lebanon, the original slips of which were said
to have been brought from the Holy Land by the Jesuit Fathers.
Apparently twisted and wrenched by time and tempest, they
present a curious appearance, with their short, gnarled trunks,
surmounted by spreading masses of dark green foliage so flattened
down as to be impervious to sunshine or rain. Only in Dore's
pictures are such trees elsewhere seen. After the drive, the
welcome banquet, and then a restful interval, followed by a lively
ball, the first magical suggestion of which dispelled the weariness
with which, down to that moment, the feminine element of the
party had been nearly overcome. And that lovely evening! Midwinter though it was, the air was soft and balmy, and redolent

with the delicious odors of a myriad beds of flowers. A mild zephyr from the Pacific imparted a tremulous motion to the everywhere overhanging foliage, through which the rays of the moon quivered and flickered in fitful flashes to the earth. Nature's repose is her most inviting aspect. The temptation for a mid-night stroll was irresistible, and, too, the lights in the Club House near by beamed with such hospitable suggestion !

Early on Sunday morning we reluctantly left Monterey, feeling, as we felt at departing from each place we visited, that the glory of the journey was over, and that the future had little to offer in comparison with past enjoyments—a feeling, by the way, which evaporated with corresponding regularity within thirty minutes after each place had passed from sight. Arriving in two hours at Santa Cruz, we were driven out to what some called the Natural Bridge, where we found a seaside observatory on a rocky point at the end of a cable road, and where we were regaled with grapes and wine, besides which some enthusiasts claimed to have had a momentary sight of a veritable Pacific Ocean whale, "spouting" in the sea. On our return to the town we were transferred to a narrow gauge branch of the Southern Pacific Railroad, and in the course of half an hour's climb up the Santa Cruz Mountains we were

OBSERVATORY AT THE NATURAL BRIDGE, SANTA CRUZ.

at "Big Tree Station," inspecting with great satisfaction a grove of colossal redwood forest monarchs. These are not the famous "big trees" of Calaveras and Mariposa, but they are plenty big enough to justify the name they bear and to be entitled to fame on their own account, one specimen having a diameter of twenty feet and an alleged height of over three hundred. As Emerson says, "they have a monstrous talent for being tall." They belong to the species *sequoia sempervirens*, and, like their larger cousins, the *sequoia gigantea*, of the Sierra Nevadas, they are regarded by scientific know-alls as survivals of a period of the world's history when, with the prevalence of a more humid atmosphere than now obtains, they were widely distributed, the fossil remains of some of them having been found as far north as the frozen soil of Greenland. The name *Sequoia* was that of an ingenious Cherokee Indian, who invented the Cherokee alphabet, and it was bestowed upon the Californian redwood by a German botanist, Endlicher, in 1847, about five years before the Calaveras grove was discovered. But the redwood is a favorite tree in California, being admirably adapted for cabinet work and general building purposes, and these majestic relics of an uncertain antiquity are rapidly disappearing before a foe more promptly destructive than the diminishing humidity of the atmosphere. The big redwood grove near Santa Cruz is justly regarded as one of the most interesting features of that picturesque coast range region. One veteran, whose trunk near the earth has been hollowed out by fire, would give comfortable standing room to fully thirty persons in its charred interior, and there are others in the grove yet larger. Having bestowed due admiration upon the big trees, we speeded on to San Jose, the capital of Santa Clara County, where we were received with enthusiastic welcome by a committee of citizens, who escorted us in fine style to most agreeable quarters in the handsome hostelry, the Hotel Vendome, which was gorgeously decorated with flowers in our honor. Luncheon was succeeded by a processional drive through the city and its suburbs, which we found resplendent with Queen Anne cottages and other tasteful residences, surrounded with fine lawns and well tended

THE LICK OBSERVATORY ON MOUNT HAMILTON, NEAR SAN JOSE, CAL.

orchards. Altogether, San Jose gave the impression of a successful little city, in which modern ideas of thrift and architecture are rapidly replacing the crudeness of earlier days. The broad streets are traversed by electric railways and are made attractive to the sight by the frequent occurrence of open squares abounding in ornamental palms. After a view of the old Mission Church and a visit to the rooms of the Board of Trade and other prominent places of interest, we returned at dusk to the Vendome to prepare for the evening's banquet, which proved to be a genuinely elegant affair. The entertainment wound up with a concert in the music hall of the hotel, and about midnight the travelers eagerly sought their apartments, thoroughly worn out with the labors of that busily occupied Sabbath. The day had been spent in verdant forests and amid blooming flowers. Just one week previous we had been sleighing at Leadville and bathing in a blinding snowstorm in the hot pool at Glenwood, Colorado. It was difficult to bring one's mind to a realizing sense of the striking experiences we had passed through in that short interval of time.

The next morning showed the Eastern party to be somewhat divided in purpose. They were universally agreed, however, that it was necessary to wire their home offices at once for a fresh supply of adjectives expressive of admiration, the stock with which they started having been completely exhausted. A large number set out at seven o'clock in carriages for a mountain climb of twenty-eight miles, to visit the Lick Observatory, on Mount Hamilton, escorted by the Mayor and a special committee. The others, contenting themselves with a distant sight of the Observatory, where

"On yon peak against the cloudless sky,
"The guarding eye of science reads the deep,"

in full view from the city, saved themselves the labor of the mountain ascent, and returned to San Francisco in the early forenoon. The party who made the Mount Hamilton trip had a glorious ride. The atmosphere was transparently clear, and the beauties of the Santa Clara Valley were unfolded in all their glory of verdant undulation, as the spirited, four-horse teams speeded along the winding road that connects the low land with the clouds. Mayor Rucker, of San Jose, the indefatigable Charles Shortridge, editor of the San Jose *Mercury*, and their associate committeemen, in collusion with the Vendome Hotel management, had sent a corps of waiters in advance with the material for a robust lunch, which was attacked and successfully overcome at Smith's Creek, a few miles below the summit of the mountain. About one o'clock, at an altitude of 4,400 feet, the great Observatory was reached, and the travelers at once laid aside all concern for earthly matters. Peering through a twelve-inch telescope, a twinkling light was indicated to them as the star Vega, many million miles more distant from them than the sun; so far away, indeed, that it requires sixteen years for a wave of its light to be transmitted to the earth. The contemplation of this mysteriously remote orb giving rise to uncomfortable suggestions as to the distance that intervened between them and heaven, they turned for comfort to the great instrument sixty feet long, with a thirty-six inch lens, that showed them Venus, which their educated minds recognized as being in much closer proximity. The wonderful mechanism of the Observatory's great dome was greatly admired, its one hundred tons of weight being so delicately poised on wheels as to revolve readily under the impetus of a moderate shove of the shoulders. The huge telescope, also, is so accurately adjusted, that it can be moved with the pressure of one's hand. Every imaginable contrivance of mechanical ingenuity requisite for carrying into effect the purposes of the institution's founder appears to have been provided for that little colony of star-gazers, whose thirty or

THREE OF THE FOUNDERS OF THE INTERNATIONAL LEAGUE OF PRESS CLUBS.

FOSTER COATES.   THOMAS H. KEENAN, JR.   LYNN R. MEEKINS.

forty members are supplied with food from San Jose, twenty-eight miles away, and who, when snow obstructs the mountain roads, are wholly cut off from intercourse with the outside world. The descent of the mountain was accomplished with exhilarating rapidity, and at half-past six o'clock the party were in San Francisco with time to dine and rest before preparing for the entertainment of the evening.

That night marked an epoch in the life of every member of the party. The men were the guests of the San Francisco Press Club at a banquet in the Palace Hotel, and the ladies were given a reception by the Pacific Coast Women's Press Association at the Pleasanton Hotel. Both were memorable events. The steady succession of agreeable surprises that had marked the entertainments during the week had inspired the Eastern party with a profound admiration for the capacity for hospitality possessed by their San Francisco Press Club hosts. The Palace Hotel farewell banquet was a fitting culmination of the series, though in some respects it seemed calculated to result in retarding the parting guests rather than to speed them on their way. At the main table Mr. Hugh Hume, President of the San Francisco Press Club, presided, with Gen. W. H. L. Barnes at his right as toast-master. Next to the last named gentleman was General Ruger, the popular commander of the Military Department of the Pacific; and interspersed among the guests at the table, and at the five others that extended from it at right angles, were many local celebrities, representing the bar, the press and the municipal government. The unique *menu* card deserves to be perpetuated. It comprised several pages in imitation of "copy" prepared for printing, fastened together at the upper end with a cord. On the first page was depicted a bear, holding in one paw a bottle of ink taken from an open box labeled "The Press Club of San Francisco." In the background, in letters of gold, was the inscription, "International League of Press Clubs," while underneath the whole were the words, "Report of the Committee on Banquet tendered to the visiting delegates of the International League of Press Clubs, San Francisco, January 18th, 1892." The *menu* was as follows:

To the President and Board of Managers, San Francisco Press Club:

GENTLEMEN.—The committee appointed by you in the matter of the banquet for the visiting delegates report as follows:

After a certain amount of highly respectable discussion, it was decided to hold the banquet at the Palace Hotel. There are, of course, many finer and more pretentious hostelries than this in our city and vicinity, but this strikes a fair average and will give our visitors something of an idea how the San Francisco newspaper man lives during 365 days in the year.

The Courses — • • •

Which is the most elegant Anglo-Saxon we could extract from M-E-N-U, we are happy to say, have been determined upon without serious collision between any of the committeemen, but you will never know the amount of gray matter expended in the elaboration of the M-E-N-U. (Your next banquet committee will learn of it through sad experience.) We have decided to commence with

California Oysters.—This will put our guests at home immediately and will give them an opportunity of remarking how superior our bivalve is to that of the effete East. After this succulent product of our native heath (?) comes

Consomme (*Royal*)—This is as near as we could come to straight English, as there appeared to be a lack of euphony about "royal soup."

Hors D'Oeuvres (*Assorted*)—There was considerable silence regarding this item. Only one member appeared familiar with the subject, and even he admitted that there was some doubt in his mind as to whether what he had once partaken of was *hors d'oeuvres* or *hors de combat*.

Kennebec Salmon (*Holland Sauce*), POTATOES PARISIAN.—" What's the matter with Sacramento River Salmon?" was the query immediately propounded by an obstreperous member, but it availed him nothing, as the committee were totally unfamiliar with the rights of minorities.

Sweetbreads (*St. Cloud*).—Anent this there was hot discussion, chiefly regarding the pronunciation of the qualifying adjunct. When it was learned how the majority pronounced it, the member hailing from Boston retired from active duty with the committee.

Broiled Mushrooms.—Unanimously decided upon. Even the doubting Thomas, who feared the possibility of getting something not the *agaricus campestris*, was carried away by the popular enthusiasm. After this little divertisement comes

Filet of Beef (*Richelieu*), FRENCH PEAS.—After which comes the piece of resistance (?) of the evening. (We were told it was absolutely necessary to use this expression about something or the banquet would not be complete. The ordnance editor did the translating.)

Canvas-back Duck, CELERY SAUCE.—There was some discussion as to whether the ducks should be served with or without the canvas, but on motion, duly seconded, the matter was referred back to the head cook, with power to act. After this, in rapid succession will come

Dessert.

Coffee.   **Liqueurs.**

78

SOME OF THE GUESTS OF THE PRESS CLUB LEAGUE.

MRS. DR. HUNTER,	MRS. J. H. YAGER,	MISS MATTISON,
MISS A. KELLOGG,	MRS. LYNN R. MEEKINS,	MRS. E. H. MARTIN

While the foregoing affair is being served, it is proposed that the assembled guests and occasional hosts partake of

Hock (Napa Valley Wine Company).
Haut Sauterne (Charles A. Wetmore).
Portola Vineyard Claret (E. F. Preston).
Margaux, Souvenir (Charles A. Wetmore).
Moet & Chandon, Brut Imperial.
G. H. Mumm, Extra Dry.

By way of parenthesis, we wish to state that it has been your committee's sole and constant aim to please those who want the earth. Providence alone knows how near we have come to it.

A trifle weary and travel-stained, and with sincere sympathy for the concocters of the next banquet, we beg to submit ourselves, your obedient servants.

THE COMMITTEE.

The parenthetical allusion to those who wanted " the earth " was, of course, intended for home application exclusively. The Eastern delegates on that evening would have been contented to take San Francisco as their modest share. The speeches that followed the discussion of the repast have been officially recorded in the annual report of the League, and it only remains to state here that throughout the night and until the small hours of the morrow the reason of the diners was copiously feasted while their souls overflowed with the inspiring influences of good fellowship and good cheer.

The Ladies' Reception given by the Women's Press Association, of California, at the Hotel Pleasanton, was an equally brilliant and successful affair. There were some outspoken denunciations of the exclusiveness of the men's banquet, whereby was enforced a separation of the sexes wholly out of harmony with the professed principles of the League, but on the whole the ladies proved equal to the emergency and made a night of it on their own account, of which they will long treasure the remembrance. The guests were received by a committee of the Club in the handsomely decorated parlors of the hotel, and as very few declinations had been received to the seven hundred and fifty invitations sent out, the committee had a tolerably busy time. The formal exercises that followed the introduction of the visitors were begun by Miss Kate Field, who spoke in warm terms of the useful functions exercised by Press Clubs in the United States, drawing a line, however, at the point where men go off to feast by themselves to the utter exclusion of their professional sisters. But the speakers who followed Miss Field were so eloquent in their eulogiums of women, and of journalistic women in particular, that the audience forgot the slight the men had offered them in rapturous contemplation of their own transcendent excellences. The reception terminated at midnight, and was voted by all the participants as having been one of the most delightful assemblages imaginable.

The ladies to whom the visitors were indebted for their agreeable entertainment comprised with others the following committees :

Programme Committee:

Mrs. Juliette Mathis,
" E. O. Smith,
" L. J. Watkins,

Mrs. Lydia Prescott,
" Alice Kingsbery Cooley,
" M. P. Johnson,

Miss Mary Lambert.

Reception:

Mrs. Lillian Plunkett,
" Jeana Achilly Neal,
Juliette Mathis,
Louise Humphrey Smith,

Mrs. Frances B. Edgerton,
" Leila Ellis,
" Mary Lynde Hoffman,
" Sarah B. Cooper,

Miss Minna V. Lewis.

Entertainment:

Mrs. Barbara Knell,
" Florence Percy Mathison,
" Alice Cary Waterman,

Mrs. F. W. D'Evelyn,
" Lillian Plunkett,
" Juliette Mathis.

Tuesday, January 19th, was devoted to concluding the business of the Convention, and after the adjournment of that body the visitors dispersed themselves over the city seeing the sights, inspecting the palaces on Nob Hill and in other localities dedicated to wealth and fashion, and in searching for mementos of the visit to carry back to their homes. For this was to be their last day in San Francisco, and despite the multifarious excitements of the preceding week it seemed to the Eastern party as though they had enjoyed too little opportunity for acquainting themselves with the characteristics of the Occidental city, whose open gates had invited them to cross the continent and of whose broad-gauged people they were always thereafter to carry so agreeable a remembrance. Accordingly, that was a busily occupied afternoon, winding up with a fine banquet at the hotel, tendered by their host of a week, Mr. Baldwin. The entire first floor of the hotel was decorated with palms, ferns, green trees, smilax and potted firs, so that the dining room was entered through a gorgeous bower.

In the evening the climax of entertainment was reached in a reception given in honor of the visiting delegates by Mr. and Mrs. M. H. de Young in their handsome residence on California street. There was a cheery informality about that last evening of the San Francisco visit, which was especially charming, and the entertainment throughout was so cordially genial as to avert from it the slightest tinge of sombreness that might be predicated of a concerted leave-taking. This effect was further sustained by the fact that the host and hostess were pledged to accompany the travelers throughout the remainder of their journey in California, an arrangement that had been greeted with unqualified satisfaction. There were over four hundred members of San Francisco's choicest society gathered in the de Young mansion, and the evening slipped merrily away. The supper down stairs in the extensive Chinese room drew forth exclamations of amazement from those who had not previously seen that wonderful apartment, with its wealth of gorgeous and grotesque splendor, cunning carvings, rare mosaics and other curiosities innumerable. Great, however, as was the admiration elicited by the varied display of Celestial skill, one, after all, could not avoid feeling a certain triumphant sense of personal superiority while sipping Ruinart and Pommery Sec, and discussing the

RECEPTION ROOM IN M. H. DE YOUNG'S RESIDENCE, SAN FRANCISCO.

elaborate menu at a table on which possibly Confucius had written the "Five Canonical Books" that for the past fourteen centuries have served as the basis of Chinese literature. Whatever the anachronism involved, the nineteenth century certainly had the best of it that evening. But midnight had long since passed, and an early start must be made on the morrow. Trunks were meanwhile to be packed and other arrangements to be perfected for the homeward journey. So with lingering grasps of the hands of our newly made friends, and mutual expressions of hopes of again meeting, the last farewells were spoken and the final entertainment in San Francisco of the Eastern delegates was ended.

It would be out of place, if, indeed, it were practicable, to refer by name to every person to whom the visitors had been indebted for courtesies and hospitalities during their visit to San Francisco. To the Press Club Reception Committee, however, the writer desires to record, for himself and on behalf of his associates and traveling companions, some faint sense of the unqualified gratification which the unwearying attentions of that committee afforded, and to repeat here the wish, that had a thousand utterances before the party broke up at the journey's end, that it may be their pleasure and happiness some day to act in their turn as the hosts and entertainers of those noblemen of the Pacific Slope. The committee in question comprised Gen. John F. Sheehan, Chairman; Hugh Hume, President of the San Francisco Press Club; O. Black, Secretary; M. H. de Young, Local Delegate to the League of Press Clubs; T. T. Williams, Ross Jackson, John McComb, H. H. Egbert, E. A. Phillips, John Finlay, Harry Mann, Judge Hunt, T. F. Bonnet, Harry M. Tod, O. J. Stillwell, E. F. Moran, Samuel Ewing, Samuel Davis, T. J. Murphy, Jeremiah Lynch, C. M. Palmer, John Lord Love, George R. Sanderson, James O. Denny, Nat J. Brittan and E. W. Townsend.

The San Francisco Press Club had, as already shown, welcomed us on our arrival in glowing words of tempting invitation. Their farewell dirge was equally characteristic :

" The newspaper men of San Francisco say good-bye to their visiting brethren of the East with reluctance. The association has done us good; and, if we were able, we would hold you

84

here for a fortnight longer. We are heartily glad to know you, and there is enough testimony in to warrant the belief that the occasion has not been wholly devoid of interest to yourselves.

"But the fiat of the autocratic body known as the Committee of Arrangements has gone forth, and you must leave us. May your homeward journey be safe, and may you carry with you a pleasant recollection of California and her people. Though you have seen a deal of California and Californians since your entrance into the State, there is still in store for you much which has never, up to date, failed to attract and hold the interest of the Eastern visitor. That semi-tropical wonderland of the South, the land of golden fruits and blossoming flowers and singing birds, the Italy of America, remains to be explored. At Fresno, where you are programmed for a day's stay, you will be shown the world's largest and finest raisin vineyards, and gain an idea of the nature of our interior midwinter climate.

"For one hundred and fifty miles from Fresno your route lies through the great San Joaquin Valley, and then, crossing Tehachapi, some of the difficulties which beset the Southern Pacific Company will be noted. Then comes the Mojave desert; it is a novelty, but we are not proud of it.

"Then comes Los Angeles, the metropolis of the Southern citrus belt. Here is the earliest home (in California) of the orange, the lemon, the fig and the vine; the bananas and pineapples are now on the list.

"Then come Riverside, San Bernardino and San Diego, all replete with glories due to Nature's bounteous blessing of soil and climate.

"Then there is a climb over the mountains, another desert to cross and the thing is done. You have left California and are on your way home.

"Good-by! Come again.

"THE PRESS CLUB OF SAN FRANCISCO."

If any point of this narrative sustains the inference that while in California the visitors had been afforded the privilege of resting, the writer has failed to express himself as lucidly as he had desired. Such a concession by the San Francisco Press Club

85

would have been a clear violation of contract on the part of that organization. At a dinner at the Marlborough Hotel, in New York, given the previous November by members of the New York Press Club to the visiting officers of the League, Mr. de Young, in inviting the delegates to visit the Pacific Slope, distinctly stated that he was instructed by the San Francisco Press Club to promise the visitors during their stay a full supply of everything, excepting sleep. That promise, with its limitation, was kept to the letter. They evidently thought it would be superfluous for the visitors to lie in bed, when opportunities were so abundant elsewhere. The only other luxury, besides that of sleep, which was at all sparingly offered was drinking water. But, in fairness to San Francisco, it should be borne in mind that the visit was made during the "rainy season," when no special provision of that element would seem to be required. However, if the visitors suffered any particular inconvenience from the deprivation, they were politely careful not to allude to it in the face of the masterly example of abstinence set them by their hosts.

Wednesday, January 20th, marked a new epoch in the journey. Invitations had been received from several cities in the southern part of the State, through the municipal authorities and boards of trade and citizens' committees, for the Eastern delegates to visit them on their homeward journey, and the Southern Pacific Railroad, which had captured us at Ogden, insisted upon holding us in its grasp until we should arrive at Los Angeles. Accordingly, after parting with some of our San Francisco hosts at the hotel, and being escorted across the ferry to Oakland by others, we started from the depot in the latter place at 10 o'clock on Wednesday morning, having first arrived in that city on the afternoon of the Wednesday previous. At 2 P. M. we reached Sacramento in the custody of Messrs. Houghton, Davis, Sheehan,

Schmidt, Larkin and Drury, a committee of representatives of that
capital, who had joined the train at Davisville. The delegates
were presented with printed programmes descriptive of the city.
Mayor Comstock, with other committeemen, received us at the
depot, and we were speedily driven to the rooms of the Sutter
Club, where a bevy of particularly handsome lasses were waiting
to assist us to an elegant luncheon, after presenting the men of
the party with boutonnieres of violets and the ladies with corsage
bouquets. Several brief addresses followed on both sides, Mr. S.
Prentiss Smith and Mayor Comstock speaking in behalf of
Sacramento, and Messrs. de Young, Berri and Worrall for the
League. Mr. de Young's eloquent acknowledgment of Sacramento's splendid reception of the delegates was vigorously indorsed
by the latter body, and, after a most agreeable entertainment, the
party re-entered their carriages and were conveyed to the State
Capitol building, where Secretary Johnson did the honors in the
absence of Governor Markham, who was detained at home by an
attack of the grip. After inspecting the Capitol, under the escort
of a joint committee of citizens and pretty girls, a reception was
held in the Assembly Chamber. Attorney-General Hart greeted
the visitors in words of warm welcome, to which President de
Young responded in felicitous phrases. Ex-Vice-President Lynn
R. Meekins, of Baltimore, followed with a masterly speech that
was roundly applauded, and Messrs. Page and Berri, of New York,
also spoke with effect. From the Capitol the guests were given
an opportunity to examine the paintings in the million dollar
Crocker Art Gallery, and were subsequently taken to Sutter's Fort
and through the principal streets of the city. A conspicuous
feature of the entertainment in Sacramento, one over which the
young unmarried men of the party were agitated for days afterwards, and which, strange to say, even the ladies of the party

cordially conceded, was the presence among the entertainers of a number of especially pretty and lovable young ladies. Sacramento, on account of such a revelation of loveliness, will always have a warm place in the remembrance of that Eastern party. It was with unfeigned reluctance that the train was taken at 7 in the evening, for it seemed that it would have been pleasant to spend a week in Sacramento rather than to hurry through the place in the brief hours of a midwinter afternoon.

CHAPTER III.

SOUTHERN CALIFORNIA.

JANUARY 21-24, 1892.

ITH the early morning of January 21st began the party's delightful experience of Southern California, the Italy of America. It lasted but four short days, but it implanted pleasant memories to endure through the lifetime of all who shared it. Waking at Fresno on Thursday the day was devoted to visiting and inspecting the vineyards, including Col. William Forsyth's raisin vineyards and the wine cellars, that abound in the vicinity of that enterprising and go-ahead community. Friday was devoted to Pasadena and Los Angeles, driving through and around the former, and at the latter, where some of the party were entertained by Mr. D. Freeman, a friend of Mr. de Young, with a unique Spanish breakfast, the delegates dined in royal style in the open air under the shadow of orange and pepper trees on the spacious lawns of Judge Silent's residence, ending the day with a formal banquet at the Redondo Beach Hotel, where it was decided by unanimous vote that more comfort and satisfaction were procurable to the square inch than at any watering place on the Atlantic coast. Saturday the orange groves of Redlands were visited, where the roads traversed miles and miles of orchards fairly groaning

89

beneath their golden burden of luscious fruit, the overladen
branches being sustained by poles to prevent their breaking. At
San Bernardino lunch was partaken of and speeches were delivered,
after which the party were hastened to Riverside, where they
enjoyed a fifteen mile drive over the splendid roads and through
the unspeakably beautiful Magnolia Avenue, resuming their journey
at 7.30 in the evening. On Sunday morning, January 24th, at

THE NEW YORK PRESS CLUB DELEGATES AT JUDGE SILENT'S, LOS ANGELES, CAL.

8.45, the southern limit of the journey was attained when the
train drew up at the depot in San Diego. A committee was in
waiting with a steamboat to take the party on an excursion down
the Bay, visiting en route the U. S. Cruiser *San Francisco*, on the
invitation of Admiral Brown, and bringing up at the Coronado
Beach Hotel, where a delightful lunch was partaken of. Some of

the party to whom steamboat rides and the quarter decks of war
vessels were no particular novelty had declined the invitation to
sail on the Bay, preferring to explore the features of interest in
and around San Diego. They were amply repaid. A cable road
shot them quickly up to a lofty summit, from which a charming
view was gained of the peaceful old Spanish valley, while the
ancient town lay spread beneath them, and beyond it the lovely
Bay, whose unruffled surface was in peaceful keeping with the
Sabbath stillness that on every side prevailed. A short carriage ride
brought the visitors to the old Mission, whose bell has echoed
through that Valley for more than two centuries, and a little
further to a small adobe cottage, immortalized by Helen Hunt as
the house in which her heroine, Ramona, was wedded to her Indian
lover. The streets of San Diego were also quaintly attractive, but
as the stores were all closed, the temptations of their windows were
a vain display. Later in the afternoon a reception was given the
visitors in the San Diego Opera House, and at 6 p. m. the train
set out once more to cross the Continent, this time traveling
eastward. Nearly 4,800 miles had been already traveled, and a
week's journey was still before them.

In thus rapidly summarizing the trip through Southern
California the enjoyments that attended it have hardly been hinted
at. The experience was a new one to nearly every person in the
party. The weather was deliciously clear, and the soft, balmy air
of that half-tropical region in the middle of January, and the fruits
and flowers and brilliant foliage that were found abounding on
every hand, were a revelation for which even the phenomena they
had encountered during the previous ten days of Pacific Coast life
had scarcely prepared them. Some of the more marked events of
those four days of sunshine and pleasure demand recognition. So,
also, does the delightful climate that had favored us so admirably

throughout. California climate is one of those things that has to be experienced to be appreciated, or even understood. California presents all the features of the temperate and the semi-tropic zones. Upon the mountain heights eternal snow looks down. In the great valleys of the Santa Clara, Sacramento and San Joaquin, the flowers ever bloom. Upon the coast the chilly sea breeze blows. In the interior valleys, summer suns descend and an almost tropical warmth exists which causes vegetation to grow in a way that is wonderful to behold. The famous Japan Current, anti-type of the Atlantic Gulf Stream, sweeps the coast, and in winter its warm breath extends inland to the Sierra Nevadas, making the weather mild and the rains warm. Fogs seldom exist, except along the coast. There are a few hot days in summer, we were told, in the interior, but the nights are nearly always cool and pleasant. During nine months in the year the weather is about perfect. There are only two seasons in California, the wet and the dry. The rainfall in winter is very light, and rain in summer or between April and November is hardly known. The dry atmosphere makes the heat of the interior valleys bearable, and it is a well known fact that a temperature from fifteen to twenty degrees higher than that to which one is accustomed in the East may be borne with comfort. There is scarcely a day in the year when the weather is so warm or so cold as to prevent a person in good health from working out in the open air. Dr. Remondino, of San Diego, in his instructive book on "The Mediterranean Shores of America," discussing Southern California in relation to its climatic, physical and meteorological conditions, finds there six distinct classes of climate, all having their characteristic therapeutic advantages. "These are the purely insular climate, the peninsular, the coast, the foot-hill and valley, ranging in elevation from 200 to 2,500 feet above sea level, the mountain climate, from 2,500 feet to 9,000 feet elevation, and the desert climate, from 360 feet below sea level to 2,500 feet above." With such a well defined variety to select from everybody ought to be accommodated to his taste and satisfaction. A special characteristic also, of the Southern California climate is its tonic, bracing quality. It has often been compared to that of Italy, but the comparison is inexact, for it is wholly devoid of the unpleasant peculiarities of the Italian

UTILIZING A BRIEF HALT AT A WINE HOUSE NEAR FRESNO, CAL.

climate, which latter has the pernicious effect of indisposing people to physical or mental effort. In California life is wide-awake and active, laziness is exotic. Well has it been said that "in that refulgent summer it is a luxury to draw the breath of life."

Returning to our entrance into Southern California after leaving Sacramento, the insight into grape culture and the wine

93

industry gained at Fresno was of great interest. The party, breaking into several detachments, visited, as has been stated, all the leading vineyards in the vicinity, and the recollection of the hospitality they received at Barton's, Woodworth's, Egger's, Eisen's and Forsyth's will long be cherished. Fresno, with its crowded streets and busy stores, impressed them as a wonderfully active place, especially when they learned that it had grown from 600 to 14,000 in population during the past ten years. After the luncheon at the Hughes House, Mr. Marcus Pollasky announced that there was to be no speech-making on that occasion, whereupon an hour or so was devoted to making speeches. Dr. Chester Rowell welcomed the guests in a very neat address, and, after the statistics of Fresno County had been exhaustively rehearsed, Mr. M. H. de Young gave the citizens of Fresno some practical advice relative to developing the county's resources by introducing canals and rendering the San Joaquin River navigable, which advice was received with manifest approval. Messrs. Wilde, Martin and Page also addressed the gathering. One distinctive feature of Fresno in which its people take justifiable pride is its claim to the possession of "the finest opera house of any city in America of less than 100,000 population." An inspection of the establishment gave the impression that the claim is not an idle boast. An impromptu entertainment was at once started, Mrs. Frank Leslie leading the way with a recitation of the stirring Columbus ode "Sail On," followed by Miss Kate Field and Marshall P. Wilder.

At Pasadena, on the following day, new charms were brought to view. Orange groves loaded down with golden spheres stretched out on every hand, dotted with cottages and lawns, and back of all snow-capped mountains. Riding in any direction every turn in the road revealed new beauties. Pasadena is the chosen home of the wealthy, and the residences and surroundings bear evidence of large purses and lavish expenditure. The profusion of flowers threw the visitors from the Atlantic Coast into ecstasies. The handsome cottages were embowered in the dark green foliage of orange trees, and the gardens were resplendent with brilliant flowers of every possible hue. The valley view from the Raymond Hotel, stretching from the distant ocean to the mountains, is one of surpassing beauty. The party were fortunate in having selected the winter season for visiting Southern California, for at that time of the year that region is most charming, and nature's gifts are most abundantly exhibited. Mr. Charles F. Nordhoff, of the New York *Herald*, whom we met later at the Coronado Beach Hotel, relates the following experience of a January day in that region:

A PASADENA RESIDENCE.

"As I drove out from Los Angeles into the country on a January morning with a friend, we met a farmer coming into town with a market wagon of produce. It was a cloudless, warm, sunny day. The farmer's little girl sat on the seat with him, a chubby, blue-eyed little tot, with her sun bonnet half hiding her curls, and a shawl, which her careful mother had wrapped about her shoulders, carelessly flung aside. To me, fresh from the snowy plains and Sierras, and with the chill breath of winter still on me, this was a pleasing and novel sight; but the contents of the man's wagon were still more startling to my Northern eyes. He was carrying to market oranges, pumpkins, a lamb, corn, green peas in their pods, sugar-cane, lemons and strawberries. What a mixture of Northern and Southern products! What an odd and wonderful January gathering in a farmer's wagon! . . . All the fence corners, where there were fences, were crowded with the castor oil plant, which is here a perennial, twenty feet high, a weed whose brilliant crimson seed pods shine like jewels in the sunlight.

Below us as we looked off a hill-top lay the suburbs of Los Angeles, green with the deep green of orange groves and golden to the nearer view with their abundant fruit. Twenty-one different kinds of flowers were blooming in the open air in a friend's garden in the town this January day; among them the tube-rose, the jessamine and the fragrant stock or gillyflower, which has here a woody stalk, often four inches in diameter, and is, of course, a perennial. The heliotrope is trained over piazzas to the height of twenty feet, and, though the apple and pear orchards, as well as those of the almond and English walnut, will continue bare for some time, and the vineyards, just getting pruned, look dreary, the vegetable gardens are green as with us in June, and men and boys are gathering the orange crop."

The *al fresco* dinner under the pepper trees on Judge Silent's lawn in Los Angeles was a charming affair, and, with its numerous apparent incongruities to the Eastern minds of season and locality, would have stood for an Arabian Night's entertainment, held in the daytime. Oriental magic could have easily overcome that latter trifling incompatibility. Los Angeles is said to owe much of its attractiveness to its agreeable surroundings. Certainly the afternoon and evening spent at Rodondo Beach tended to verify that assertion. Among the profusion of flowers at the hotel, which the visitors were graciously invited to help themselves to, were some of the most splendid roses seen on the entire trip. The view from the hotel porch of the sun setting on the Pacific horizon was a fitting termination to a day that had been replete with brilliant and picturesque incident. Los Angeles is situated nearly in the center of one of the richest valleys on this continent. All the citrus family flourishes there to the highest perfection, and horticulture and agriculture are sustained to a degree unsurpassed anywhere. Between five and six thousand carloads of oranges, we were informed, are annually exported thence to Eastern markets, and an equal amount of transportation is required for carrying the crops of dried fruits, raisins, walnuts, wines and potatoes. In

WATCHING THE SUN SET IN THE PACIFIC OCEAN AT REDONDO BEACH.

endowments, it might compete for the championship with "The Happy Valley" which the imagination of Dr. Johnson created for the admiration of the youth of several generations ago, before the advent of Horatio Alger, Jr., or the evolution of the dime novel.

The day at Redlands was one of California's perfect winter days, too warm for wraps, but thoroughly delightful. As the visitors were driven through the stretches of orange groves they were profuse in their expressions of delight, but when Canyon Crest was reached, and the entire valley spread before the vision for miles and miles, the snow-covered tops of Old Baldy, Grayback and San Jacinto glistening in the warm sunlight, they began to realize the full force of California's wondrous scenery and climate, and were silent in their admiration. When the carriages returned to the depot they were laden with flowers and oranges, and Redlands was pronounced the choicest section of California that the party had seen, that, of course, being the regular verdict passed upon each successive town they visited. Arriving at San Bernardino –" San Berdoo," as the inhabitants call it—the Eastern guests were given a drive over the city, and were afterward entertained with a banquet at the Stewart hotel, at which 150 persons sat down. After the solids had disappeared, Judge George E. Otis welcomed the party in a brief speech, and introduced Judge Willis, who responded to the toast "The Press." He was followed by W. A. Harris, in a neat and short address, and Judge Rowell, who gave some statistics regarding the county. Marshall P. Wilder told a story or two, and Mrs. Frank Leslie recited a poem. The banquet was hurried, but successful. The train left San Bernardino at 2.30 P. M. for Riverside. In the San Bernardino range of mountains in this region, on the summit of the Grayback, is an active glacier of dimensions little inferior to some of the minor glaciers of the Alps and the Andes. The existence of this stupendous marvel of moving ice, after having been maintained but not generally believed for half a century, was, in June, 1892, verified by an expedition of scientists from Los Angeles, who discovered at a height of over 10,000 feet a frozen river a mile long and twenty-two feet in depth that is crushing down towards the valley at the rate of about forty-seven feet yearly. The day was wound up at Riverside, a town then of about 6,000 inhabitants, and possibly by the time of this writing having twice that number, so rapidly do California communities grow when they once take a start. The town owes its existence and prosperity wholly to irrigation, the water of the Santa Ana River having been distributed over an area of about fifty-two square miles, converting an arid desert into an Eden. Riverside is peculiarly an orange city. It covers a large plateau for the most part unbroken by hill or ravine. Some fifteen or twenty thousand acres of this land have been brought under cultivation, about fifteen thousand acres being devoted to citrus fruits. The land is subdivided and owned in small holdings of from five to twenty acres each, and orchard flanks orchard in solid phalanx for miles in all directions. One vast forest of orange trees covers the plain, unbroken, in most part, save by streets or the small plats devoted to residences and ornamental shrubbery. Magnolia avenue extends for many miles,

THE CORONADO HOTEL, NEAR SAN DIEGO, CAL.

being a double drive 125 feet in width, with rows of evergreen shade trees in the center and on either side. Other streets in all other cities fade in comparison with this. The drive that afternoon through Magnolia avenue was most charming. On returning to the depot specimens were obtained of genuine "American tin" from the near-by Temescal mines, and for days afterward the cars were decorated with branches of Riverside oranges. Twelve hours on the cars brought the party to San Diego, with the consequences already briefly related. The Coronado Beach Hotel is probably the largest caravansary in America; and all its appointments are most luxurious, and to travelers on the wing, as we were, most temptingly inviting. After lunching there, the party disbanded for a short time, some going to the swimming baths, others to the ball-room to listen to the music of the U. S. S. *San Francisco's* band, and later the entire party was formally escorted through the hotel and grounds. They were surprised and delighted. Of course, in such a hasty inspection only the more striking features of the place were seen, but they fully bore out the description Charles Dudley Warner gives of the Coronado in his book, "The American Italy." Mr. Warner says:

"The stranger, when he first comes upon this novel hotel and this marvelous scene of natural and created beauty, is apt to exhaust his superlatives. I hesitate to attempt to describe this hotel, this airy and picturesque and half-bizarre wooden creation of the architect. Taking it and its situation together, I know nothing else in the world with which to compare it, and I have never seen any other which so surprised at first, that so improved on a two weeks' acquaintance, and that has left in the mind an impression so entirely agreeable. It covers about four and a half acres of ground, including an inner court of about an acre, the rich made soil of which is raised to the level of the main floor. The house surrounds this, in the Spanish mode of building, with a series of galleries, so that most of the suites of rooms have a double outlook, one upon this lovely garden, the other upon the ocean or the harbor. The effect of this interior court or *patio* is to give gaiety and an air of friendliness to the place, brilliant as it is with flowers and climbing vines; and when the royal and date palms that are vigorously thriving in it attain their growth it will be magnificent. Big hotels and caravansaries are usually tiresome, unfriendly places; and if I should lay too much stress upon the vast dining-room (which has a floor area of 10,000 feet, without post or pillar), or the beautiful breakfast room, or the circular ball-room (which has an area of 11,000 feet, with its timber roof

open to the lofty observatory), or the music-room, billiard-room
for ladies, the reading-rooms and parlors, the pretty gallery
overlooking the spacious office rotunda, and then say that the
whole is illuminated with electric lights, and capable of being
heated to any temperature desired, I might convey a false
impression as to the actual comfort and homelikeness of this
charming place. On the seaside the broad galleries of each story
are shut in by glass, which can be opened to admit, or shut to
exclude, the fresh ocean breeze. Whatever the temperature
outside, those great galleries are always agreeable for lounging or
promenading. For me, I never tire of the sea and its changing
color and movement. If this great house were filled with guests,
so spacious are its lounging places, I should think it would never
appear to be crowded; and if it were nearly empty, so admirably
are the rooms contrived for family life, it will not seem lonesome.
I shall add that the management is of the sort that makes the
guests feel at home and at rest. Flowers, brought in from the
gardens and nurseries, are everywhere in profusion on the dining
tables, in the rooms, all about the house. So abundantly are they
produced that no amount of culling seems to make an impression
upon their mass."

After inspecting the hotel, the League party were re-escorted
across the Bay to San Diego, and were taken on a ride about the
city and out on the hills. Fisher's opera house was thrown open
for their inspection and admiration. A reception at the parlors of
the Hotel Brewster having been announced for five o'clock, all
assembled there at that hour, where they met the representative
people of the city. One of the most pleasing features of the
reception, though entirely impromptu, was the introduction of the
newsboys by Captain Friend. The boys listened with marked
attention to the remarks of Miss Kate Field and Mr. de Young.
At 5.30 the visitors left the Brewster for the train, and on their
arrival they found the newsboys arranged in line at the station,
who received them with cheers. Miss Kate Field then demanded
the boutonieres of the party, and off they came from broadcloth and

satin, and with her own hands Miss Field pinned them on the little fellows' jackets, after which graceful act, which set the urchins to grinning like Cheshire cats, Mrs. Frank Leslie addressed the boys briefly, but feelingly, and promised to "write up" the reception they had given the Eastern travelers. She was followed by Mr. de Young, who gave the lads a fatherly talk, which seemed to impress them. As the train moved out from the depot the crowd on the platform cheered to the echo and was vigorously answered by the departing visitors, the ladies joining in waving their handkerchiefs. That was our final adieu to the Pacific coast, and to the garden region of Southern California. Our faces were now set toward the Atlantic.

CHAPTER IV.
THE JOURNEY HOME

N LEAVING San Diego, on the night of January 24th, to set out across the continent directly for home, we took our leave of Mr. and Mrs de Young, who intended to remain a short time at Coronado Beach before returning to San Francisco. Mr. Welshons, of Pittsburg, also left us at this point, intending to extend his journey to Oregon before returning, and Mr. Koenig, of Chicago, likewise abandoned us here, as he contemplated taking ship to the Sandwich Islands. It was with no genuine good grace that the party turned their backs on the Pacific Ocean, where they had been so cordially received and so magnificently entertained. It was hard to realize that only thirteen days had elapsed since California was entered at Auburn, so many and so marked had been the events in the interval. This was the third Sunday away from home, the first having been spent in crossing the Rocky Mountains at Leadville and Glenwood, and the second at Santa Cruz and San Jose. The next was to bring us back to New York. Soon after leaving San Diego we were regaled with a treat specially gotten up for the League party by our indefatigable hosts of the Atchison, Topeka & Santa Fé Railroad, acting in collusion with the ever wide-awake Jerome. Arrangements had been made in advance for

103

illuminating the old San Juan Capistrano Mission building, situated in the Santa Ana valley, about twenty-five miles east of San Diego. This old church had been erected about 150 years previously by pious Spanish monks, who had learned, through some method of Castilian blarney, to overcome the inertia of the aboriginal inhabitants of that region and induce them to actually work, and the walls of adobe, or sun-dried bricks, seemed massive enough to have defied the elements for centuries had there not unluckily come along an earthquake in December, 1812, which destroyed the structure, besides killing thirty of its inmates. The mishap, however, heightened the present picturesqueness of the scene, as in the inky blackness of the night we viewed the shattered walls and the remains of the lofty arches by the glaring light of a huge bonfire that the devotees in charge had prepared at the instigation of the railroad officials. The effect in behalf of aesthetic satisfaction produced by seismic disturbance was impressively illustrated, and might suggest a text for some art editor to expatiate upon to advantage, as object lessons in that special branch of culture are frequently obtainable. Some time was spent at San Capistrano exploring the ruins, and examining the chapel that has been refitted for religious purposes, and the few other apartments which were sufficiently preserved to indicate the original majesty of the edifice. It is gratifying to record here the fact that the old San Capistrano Mission building has, since the date of our visit, been taken in charge by the Historical Society of Southern California, and is to be hereafter protected from the combined ravages of decay and relic-hunting vandals. A few weeks subsequent to the passage of the Press Club League, the Society named sent a party of discreet persons to thoroughly inspect the condition of the structure, and they found that a comparatively small expenditure would suffice to preserve it for many years to come. They reported on their return that "the vastness of the old Mission and the uniqueness of the architecture were a surprise to many. It was found that the large brick arches in the east and south walls of the interior court-yard were still standing almost entire, while about one-half of the north side remains. The front archways to the main building are also in a fair state of preservation, and the portion still occupied as a chapel and residence of the priest, with its coat of whitewash, presents a neat appearance. Of course, the main edifice which was destroyed by the earthquake in 1812 is almost in complete decay, but enough remains of the walls to give a fair idea of the character of the, for that time, magnificent structure. The unused rooms of the old building have a musty, sickening smell, that is almost stifling. The little chapel in use is sweet and clean, having but lately been renovated and repaired. Ancient oil paintings and statues are scattered about, as well as furniture and altar furnishings brought from Spain more than a century ago. There are candelabra of solid silver, and massive sacred emblems of pure gold. The old bells (five in number, one of them dated 1726) still hang in their places and act as solemn monitors to all hearers of their tones, as in the palmy days of yore. A picket fence has been put around the front of the building to keep cattle away, and a little cement here and there, and some new tiles on the roof in spots, will keep the building in repair a long time."

The next morning, January 25th, we found ourselves on the Mojave Desert. It must have been a most discouraging region in which to build a railroad, but the words *Santa Fe* mean "Holy Faith," and the projectors of the road that was conveying us must certainly have been inspired by the significance of the phrase. For miles, and hundreds of miles, the road runs through an arid cactus desert, dusty and repellant to the eyes and other senses.

Along a large portion of the route that day we passed by a
succession of extinct volcanos, through vast lava fields, whose hard

A MOHAVE BELLE.

material had been worn by the action of
the elements, or possibly by the erosive
action of some ancient inland sea, into all
imaginable and unimaginable shapes. The
grotesque formations that line the river
beds of the Northwest, through the region
which General Hazen immortalized as the
"Great Uncultivable American Desert," and
known locally in those regions as "Bad
Lands," were vividly suggested by the
strange and weird shapes that had been
assumed by these remains of ancient vol-
canic action, recalling General Sully's epito-

mization of the *Terres Mauvaises* as
"Hell, with the fires out." In many
places, seen at a distance lining the horizon of that dreary desert, and even closer
by as we sped rapidly past, the eye seemed
to dwell upon long ranges of human structures, forts and castles, and towers with
minarets, and formidable walled cities.
The impression of human agency in their
contrivance was pervading and irresistible.
About noon the train was stopped to allow
a confab with a band of Indians, the most
squalid, abject and repulsive masters of
the soil, probably, to be encountered on
this continent. Their long hair, ignorant
of combs, hung over their low foreheads, covering their unwashed

A MOHAVE BOW.

faces and their eyes, and giving them a fierce, animal appearance. The only sign of genuine intelligence they displayed during our brief interview with them was their emphatic disinclination to be made the victims of amateur photographers. These savages were reported to make their principal diet upon grasshoppers, and, judging from the proximity of their bones to the surface, their supplies must have been short that season. At 1 P. M. we crossed, at the Needles, from California into Arizona, and there again we stopped for some time to interview a party of Mojave Indians who were lounging about the station to give us a welcome and

MOJAVE PEDLERS AT THE NEEDLES.

to sell bows and pottery. The men were tall, and not without some semblance to good looks, a quality of which the less than half-clad squaws were utterly destitute. Time was, once, when the Mojaves were famous for their bravery and prowess; now their leading characteristics are indolence and vice. A member of our party, engaging in conversation with one of the few white men that were lounging about the station, drew from that worthy, a very good looking man, a gambler by profession, the following account of the Indians: "We had some trouble with them at first, because they insisted in coming to town dressed wholly in their conscious innocence; but we finally got together enough second-hand clothes to make them fairly respectable, though far from decent. They do the coarse work about the town, and make enough to live on." Apparently, they need as little food as raiment. So through the alkali dust and amidst wreckage of pre-historic ages we sped

steadily Eastward throughout that and the following day, until at
1.30 P. M., on January 26th, we were afforded an opportunity for
enjoying one of the most interesting experiences of the whole
homeward journey. The train was stopped at a village inhabited
by Laguna Pueblo Indians. This unique settlement was composed
of a series of adobe structures, planted on a hillside, and built one
above the other in terraces like the steps of an enormous stairway.
As originally built they had no doors, access to the interiors being
gained only by climbing to the roofs with ladders, and descending
in like manner through trap
doors. The houses in that
little community constitute one
of the greatest archaeological
curiosities of North America,
as they are accepted by ethnolo-
gists as having pertained to
some semi-civilized people that
existed, and occupied the soil,
and disappeared, wholly prior, it
is asserted, to even the advent
of the red aborigines. The

THE ANCIENT PUEBLO TOWN OF LAGUNA, N. M.

Laguna Indians of the present time have traits and habits that
distinguish them from all other tribes of Indians, their persistent
living in houses being one of the most marked of these. They
have improved upon the plans of the original architects of the
place by piercing the walls of each tier of buildings with doorways,
and our party, visiting the interiors of these curious relics of
pre-historic antiquity, were agreeably surprised at the cleanliness and
tidy order that everywhere prevailed. We visited them in their
residences, inspected their church, avoided their mangy dogs, and
pretty nearly denuded the place of all the pottery it contained,

buying for small sums some very neat and curious specimens
of Indian handicraft, quaintly designed.   The conventional price
asked for a clay image the size of one's thumb, or for a
bowl of the same material big enough for a Press Club
punch-bowl, was a quarter of a dollar, or, in the vernacular of
the Arizona desert, and of the West generally, "two-bits."   After
hearing this latter phrase constantly repeated, evidently the sum
total of Laguna's acquaintance with commercial Anglo Saxon, it
was quite startling when a comely maiden, modest and neatly
attired, turned to our party and said in excellent English, "I shall
be very glad to show you around."   It proved on investigation
that this young daughter of the desert was a graduate of the
Indian school at Carlisle, Pennsylvania.   Having been educated
after civilized fashion she had returned to her tribe.   Who knows
what destiny was before her, whether she would succeed in the
missionary work of raising her associates toward the plane to which
she herself had been raised, or whether, as unfortunately usually
happens, she would ultimately relapse into their condition ?   Pushing
onward at three o'clock, and picking up at some unknown stopping
place our old friend, Captain Jack Crawford, "The Poet Scout,"
we reached Albuquerque, which, at the depot, presented quite a
modern, almost an Eastern, appearance, but which, further on,
when the Mexican section was penetrated, showed up in the light
of an old thriftless, untidy Mexican settlement.   However, the
leaven of Eastern push has found its way there and the town,
despite the sharp line of demarcation between the two sections, is
rapidly being Americanized.   It contains some very fine buildings,
notably the hotel and the Commercial Club, and a newspaper
office, nearly completed at the time of our visit, besides electric
lights and national banks.   In New Mexico the nineteenth century
is still struggling to get the better of fifteenth century sluggishness,

but neither the present nor the next generation will witness its success. A committee from the Commercial Club drove us around through this interesting city, with which we would gladly have become more familiar. Our time was brief, however, and we were forced to hurry on, reaching Santa Fé, the famous capital of the territory, at nine o'clock in the evening, nearly eight hours behind the time set down for our arrival, owing to the delays that grew

STREET SCENE IN SANTA FÉ.—NEW MEXICAN WOOD CARRIER.

out of the interest we had felt in the several points at which we had been stopping.

At Santa Fé the Press League party received a genuine Territorial ovation. The Reception Committee had joined us at Albuquerque, and, although a little dismayed at the interruption to their plans our tardiness occasioned, they did their duty as entertainers most handsomely. A great crowd was present at the depot on our arrival, and we were bundled without delay into carriages and driven rapidly to the State House, a splendid building to find in such a locality, which had just been completed, and was brilliantly illuminated for our reception, but which was destined to be a few months afterward totally destroyed by fire. The Reception Committee rather prided themselves on this building, as well they might, for it not only was a very imposing edifice, but its whole cost had been paid for out of Territorial funds, a large portion of the surplus apportioned for that purpose having actually been turned in again to the Territorial Treasury. The general circulation of this statement made the New York delegates, especially, gaze at one another in silent, pensive wonderment. Ushered into the Legislative Chamber on the upper floor we found a large assemblage awaiting us, in the galleries, Mexicans; on the floor, army officers in full uniform, mostly pertaining to the Tenth United States Infantry, which then constituted the garrison of Santa Fé, besides handsome and handsomely dressed ladies and Eastern visitors. Gov. L. Bradford Prince, erstwhile of Long Island, made a very sprightly speech of welcome to the party, the effect of which was sensibly heightened by the commanding figure and sonorous voice of the speaker. Then the Tenth Infantry Band discoursed some patriotic airs, followed by some sweet pretty singing from the voices of about fifty Indian girls from the neighboring Ramona school, who had been awaiting our arrival for eight hours in order to give us that melodious welcome. At the conclusion of the children's singing we were shown through the building and were then rapidly transported to the "Palace," the name which the ancient edifice occupied by the Governor of the Territory has borne for many years. It is a long, one-story building facing the public square, occupied by the post-office and other government departments, a number of apartments in one end being set aside as the Governor's residence. The appearance of this ancient structure scarcely justifies the conventional suggestions of its name. It was erected in 1598, and has a certain latter-day distinction upon which much stress is laid in the circumstance of its having been occupied by General Lew Wallace while he was Governor of New Mexico, in 1879 and 1880. It was in one of the apartments of this house that he wrote his famous novel, "Ben Hur," and it was in the room in which that book was written that the Press League were received by Governor Prince and his bright and charming wife. The reception was the occasion of a large gathering of the ladies and gentlemen of Santa Fé, including the officers of the Tenth Infantry and the ladies of the garrison. The evening was passed most agreeably in conversation and in the examination of the multitude of local curiosities and old time prints and

THE PALACE, SANTA FE, N. M.

pictures which Governor Prince has gathered during his long residence in New Mexico, the Tenth Infantry Band meanwhile discoursing excellent music. Speaking of the Palace, Governor Prince declared it to be the most interesting place in the country. Certainly no other structure in America has such a history behind it. It antedates the settlement of Jamestown by nine years, and that of Plymouth by twenty-two, and has stood during the two hundred and ninety-two years, since its erection, as the living centre of everything of historic importance in the Southwest. Through all that long period, whether under Spanish, Pueblo, Mexican or American control, it has been the seat of power and authority. Whether the ruler was called Viceroy, Captain-General, Political Chief, Department Commander or Governor, and whether he presided over a kingdom, a province, a department or a territory, this has been his official residence. "From here," said Governor Prince, "Onate started in 1599 on his adventurous expedition to the Eastern plains; here, seven years later, eight hundred Indians

THE OLDEST BUILDING IN AMERICA, AT SANTA FÉ, N. M.

came from far-off Quivira to ask aid in their war with the Aztecs; from here, in 1618, Vincento de Salivar set forth to the Moqui country, only to be turned back by rumors of the giants to be encountered; and from here Penalosa and his brilliant troop started, on the 6th of March, 1662, on their marvelous expedition to the Missouri; in one of its strong rooms the commissary general of the Inquisition was imprisoned a few years later by the same Penalosa; within its walls, fortified as for a siege, the bravest of the Spaniards were massed in the revolution of 1680; here, on the 19th of August of that year, was given the order to execute forty-seven Pueblo prisoners in the plaza which faces the building; here, but a day later, was the sad war council held which determined on the evacuation of the city; here was the scene of triumph of the Pueblo chieftains as they ordered the destruction of the Spanish archives and the church ornaments in one grand conflagration; here De Vargas, on September 14th, 1692, after the eleven hours' combat of the preceding day, gave thanks to the Virgin Mary, to whose aid he attributed his triumphant capture of the city; here, more than a century later, on March 3d, 1807, Lieutenant Pike was brought before Governor Alencaster as an invader of Spanish soil; here, in 1822, the Mexican standard, with its eagle and cactus, was raised in token that New Mexico was no longer a dependency of Spain; here, on the succeeding day, Jose Gonzales, a Pueblo Indian of Taos, was installed as Governor of New Mexico, soon after to be executed by order of Armijo; here, in the principal reception room, on August 12, 1846, Captain Cooke, the American envoy, was received by Governor Armijo and sent back with a message of defiance; and here, five days later, General Kearney formally took possession of the city, and slept, after his long and weary march, on the carpeted earthen floor of the Palace." The Governor thinks the ultimate use of the building should be as a home for the antiquities of New Mexico. We slept on our train at the station that night, and early the next morning we were exploring this interesting place which enjoys the distinction of being the most ancient city of the country, and one of the most ancient capitals of the world. It is largely built of adobes, and it abounds in all kinds of interest. For instance, we went into modern stores, and from these we visited the old San Miguel church that retains a great deal of the wood used in its construction more than three hundred years ago, it having been built by the Spaniards in 1545. Near the church is an adobe house reported to be still more ancient, being, in fact, the oldest structure

built by white men in America. Then we visited the shops and laid in supplies of curios, particularly some very fine filagree work in gold and silver. Afterwards, while some of the party drove out to the Ramona school others witnessed a meek performance of guard mounting at Fort Worth, subsequently attending a concert given in honor by the Tenth Infantry Band on the plaza in front of the Palace, at the conclusion of which we resumed our places in the train, bearing away with us as guests for the rest of the day Governor

THE OLDEST CHURCH IN AMERICA,
AT SANTA FÉ, N. M.

and Mrs. Prince and several Santa Fé gentlemen and ladies.

Our visit to Santa Fé was marked, on the previous evening, by a little episode that at one time seemed likely to create some excitement, though its secret was so carefully guarded that its narration in these pages will be the first intimation of it to a majority of the League excursionists. It had been the subject of constant regretful comment among the latter that the editors of Eastern newspapers seemed to have an entirely inadequate conception of the striking character and brilliant accompaniments of the journey. With a view to rectifying this state of inappreciative apathy, an active member of the party, formerly a resident of the West, organized a little scheme that would have secured extensive Eastern editorial notice for the party could it have been successfully carried into effect. The idea was original, but its overthrow was aboriginal. It had been noticed along the journey that Marshall P. Wilder was a source of much interest to the Indians, his small figure, droll face and big laugh attracting them immediately. They would often touch him, and seemed to think it did them good, calling him "medicine man, heap head." When it was known we were to remain over night at Santa Fé, it was planned to have a party of Indians rush into the Governor's Palace during the reception, seize and carry off Marshall, announcing that they wanted him for their "medicine man," and escape with him to an Indian mud village, several miles in the country, where he would have really experienced a night with the native New Mexico Indian, with one white companion, who knew the chief of the village. The loss would have been heralded abroad in the dispatches that night, and the brave searching party which would have been organized, chiefly from the traveling scribes, armed to the teeth, would have gallantly rescued the little humorist the next morning without bloodshed, and get back in time for the train, covered with glory and New Mexico dirt and dust. Editor Frost, of the *New Mexican*, Messrs. Wilder, Austin and Penney, representing the Associated and United Press Associations, and the originator of the idea, were the only ones who knew the secret. The Governor was counted on to get out the troops, innocently, of course, and the idea was to be worked clear through with the four above mentioned sworn to secrecy for one year. But, alas; the Indians were lacking, except a few wanderers, who looked so hungry and dirty that they challenged pity instead of suggesting thoughts of danger. Ten o'clock came and the band of Indians was not forthcoming. Still, the schemers waited and hoped, with scouts out in search of fierce red men. Then, finally, Wilder began to object. He thought it would be best for him to first telegraph his father in New York, so that he would receive the dispatch before he read the awful news in the morning papers, explaining that while Marshall had been captured by the Indians, it was "all right," and they would let him go after he had told a few stories and taught them some tricks they already knew better than he did himself. At 11 o'clock (which was 1 A. M. in New York) the Indian organizers gave it up, and thus a startling sensation was spoiled. But if a band of red men had happened along that night they would have received a welcome that would have startled their native minds and appeased their most thirsty palates. No matter what their tribe, the New Mexico editor exacted a promise that they should be called Apaches, for he didn't like Apaches.

MARSHALL P. WILDER ENTERTAINING THE INDIANS AT THE NEEDLES, CAL.

We arrived in the afternoon at the "city" of Las Vegas. This commercial center of New Mexico, of which we enjoyed a hasty view, rejoices in six bright and able newspapers, and in a city hall, the only municipal building in the territory. It lies on both sides of the Rio Gallinas, which is spanned by a substantial iron bridge. The place bears numerous evidences of a go-ahead spirit among its people, the streets and residences being lighted by electric lights and gas, and street cars traversing its more important thoroughfares. But a short stop was made there, however, when we were switched on to a branch road and a ride of five miles carried us to the splendid Montezuma

117

hotel on the crest of a lofty hill, overlooking the hot springs which have made the locality famous. The Montezuma Hotel is the finest hostelry between St. Louis and the Pacific coast, and the A., T. and S. F. Railroad Company has expended many thousands of dollars to perfect every detail. The dining-room is one of the largest and most elegant on the American continent. The party amused themselves riding on *burros*, presenting thereby an appearance of indescribable dignity, inspecting the attractions of the hotel and exploring the natural beauties of the locality, winding up with a State dinner in the fine dining room, at which the regulation speeches were made on both sides, and at six o'clock we were under way again.

That night we passed through the famous Raton Tunnel, and afterward, with a powerful engine at each end of the train, on emerging into Colorado, we made a descent of sixteen hundred feet in twenty miles. Notwithstanding both engines had their driving-wheels reversed, we shot down the mountain at such a rapid rate as to cause the sparks to fly in a continuous shower through the friction of the brake shoes against the wheels of the cars. The beauties of the region were wholly lost to us in the blackness of the night, but we had more fire-works than were really enjoyable.

Nothing of special interest happened to mar the monotony of the next day's ride through Colorado, excepting the geographical fact that at 8.15 A. M. we crossed the State line into Kansas. On that evening a particularly pleasant social event was celebrated in the Windermere, which, through being exclusively occupied by married persons, had received from the irreverent bachelors of the party the appellation of " Matrimonial Car." The fact had become known that January 28th was the second anniversary of the wedding of Delegate George F. Lyon, of the New York Press Club, and

THE BOSTON PRESS CLUB DELEGATES.

F. J. Caffrey,
J. C. Munn,   W. R. Stone,
W. V. Alexander,   W. C. Grant.

DELEGATES FROM SYRACUSE, BUFFALO AND BALTIMORE

E. J. Pross,   S. G. Lamon,
                  B. R. Newins,
    E. H. O'Hara,   L. S. Sutton

his charming wife, and their friends in that car prepared to celebrate the occasion with a surprise party. Accordingly, about eight o'clock, the seats and aisles of the Windermere were suddenly crowded by an irruption from the other cars on the train, and the young couple, to their gratified astonishment, found themselves the special centers of attraction to a large assemblage, who proceeded with merry informality to offer them every friendly congratulation that the occasion could suggest. A jollier anniversary was never celebrated. There was music, and there was speech-making, of course, and a general interchange of matrimonial experiences, which, by the brilliant coloring with which it invested the connubial state, so wrought upon the tender sensibilities of the unmarried guests that they found themselves constrained, men and women, to explain the reasons that had impelled them to remain single. It would be interesting, but manifestly improper, to reveal those confidences. The whole affair was charming, as a spontaneous testimonial of friendly regard, and it will doubtless be a cherished remembrance to the couple in whose honor it was devised, as it assuredly will be an agreeable one to all the other participants.

Reaching Kansas City shortly after midnight on January 26th, we were transferred to the Wabash Railroad, parting regretfully from our courteous hosts of the Atchison, Topeka & Santa Fé Railroad, who had been our escorts since leaving Los Angeles on January 22d. During that interval we had ridden on the tracks of that mighty organization 3,701 miles, the longest run we made on any single road in the entire journey. That forenoon we reached St. Louis.

Now, when the flying party of Press Clubbers reached St. Louis, heading Eastward, on the morning of January 26th, they began to feel themselves almost at home again, and to imagine that they already could catch the scent of the Atlantic. But there were some dainty experiences still in store for them, without an account of which this narrative would be incomplete, though, were an attempt made to relate them in detail, with full accent upon all their enjoyable incidents, and with proper proportionate allowance for their varieties of elegance and novelty and enthusiastic hospitality, this volume might well swell into a series, and this modest tale of travel be expanded into the dimensions of the tail of a comet. The representative citizens of St. Louis, on the day preceding the arrival of the Wagner train, had appointed a special Reception Committee for the entertainment of the guests, and a most expert committee it proved to be, each member thereof taking special charge of a carriage load of the visitors, for whose instruction and edification he displayed unremitting solicitude. Arriving at the depot at 11.15 o'clock, the party were without delay conveyed in carriages to the Merchants' Exchange and were ceremoniously ushered into the great hall, whereupon the bulls and bears at once ceased their shouting and cavorting, and came out of the "pit" to gaze upon the faces of the interested guests. The van of the procession was led by the Reception Committee, and they marched straight for the rostrum, where sat Mayor Noonan, President Walbridge, of the City Council, Acting President Delafield, of the Merchants' Exchange, and other prominent citizens. The visitors were welcomed by Acting President Delafield on behalf of the Exchange, and Mayor Noonan for the city. Mr. Frank Gaienne and other St. Louisans also made a few remarks. They were followed on behalf of the League party by Mr. Keenan, Miss Kate Field, Mrs. Leslie and Marshall P. Wilder. After the speech-making was over, the delegation took carriages for a drive through the parks and boulevards, and then they repaired to the Fair Grounds to partake of a handsome banquet spread by the St. Louis Jockey Club, where appropriate toasts were proposed and responded to by Mayor Noonan, Secretary Price and others in the usual way. At seven o'clock that evening the tourists left for the East. The enterprise of St. Louis journalism was displayed in the wholesale interviewing with which the papers were embellished that evening and the following day. Eugene Field and Nelly Bly, especially, neither of whom was or had been in the party, were subjected to a series of interrogatories respecting the experiences they had encountered and the ideas they had picked up on the California trip, their duly recorded responses to which excited the envy of the traveling scribes, whose most brilliant imaginative flights had never soared to such an altitude of fabulous construction. The published comments, also, alleged to have been uttered by Mr. William Wilde and Mrs. Leslie Wilde and Miss Field were only equalled in vigor of inaccuracy by the utterly misleading descriptive comments published in regard to several members of the party. This almost super-mundane journalistic gift is essentially a Western aptitude, that, as everybody knows, has no equivalent in the East. It will not bear Oriental transplanting. It was, for instance, a notable fact, and one that had given rise to much expression of regret, that Col. John A. Cockerill, President of the New York Press Club, was unable to accompany the party. That trifling circumstance, however, seemed to impart a special spur to the energy with which the reporters of the San Francisco papers interviewed him at the numerous hotels he patronized during the few days of his supposititious visit to that city.

At seven o'clock we were again under way, still on the Wabash Railroad, in our luxurious Wagner palaces, whose attractiveness seemed to increase as the time we were to enjoy them diminished. After dinner the tables were removed from the dining car, and, the passengers being seated, Mr. Berri, Chairman of the New

EASTERN AND WESTERN DELEGATES AND GUESTS.

E. B. Finley,   C. C. Smith,
Sam C. Adams,   Geo. H. Lawyer

York delegation, presented, on behalf of the assembled delegates, an elegant silver salad bowl to Mr. and Mrs. Yager, accompanying the presentation with a happy little speech that admirably expressed the sentiment of the donors, and brought blushes of modest pleasure to the cheeks of the recipients. Mr. Yager thanked the party briefly, whereupon Mr. Berri proceeded, on behalf of the same constituency, to present a handsome silver set to Mr. Jerome. That modest bachelor was so overcome with emotion that he was obliged to secure the services of Miss Kate Field to give his thanks expression. Seal rings, with their initials set in diamonds, were likewise presented to Mr. Cornell, chief of the dining car, and Mr. Morrison, the conductor, who had accompanied the train through the entire journey, and to whom every person of the party was indebted for courtesies innumerable. Nor was that important functionary, the *chef*, forgotten. The recollection of many savory meals he had prepared, and the consciousness of the general increase of avoirdupois which was attributed to his skill, were testified to in the shape of a handsome scarf pin, the acceptance of which brought to his cheeks a more ruddy glow than that they bore when he was officiating over the fires of his range. A speech being insisted upon, he shuffled forward with his white cap in his hand, and explained his position in sententious style: "I's a fuss rate cook, but I ain't no actor, so you must 'scuse me from makin' a speech." We had encountered others through the previous few weeks who, like him, were "no actors," but, alas, they did not always seek to be excused.

At noon, on January 30th, we arrived at Toledo, and it seemed as though the whole city was on the alert for our reception, thanks to the efforts of the delegates from that city, Messrs. Boyle and Murphy. The Toledo visit was simply exquisite. After being formally welcomed by the Hon. Frank H. Hurd, at the

Chamber of Commerce, and listening to the sprightly response of Delegate W. V. Alexander, of Boston, a banquet was partaken of at the elegant Club House. That repast was really remarkable for its elegance, variety and profusion. The floral display was magnificent, considering the latitude and the season of the year. At every plate was a beautiful hand-painted souvenir menu. Most delightful of all, however, were the gracious courtesies of the ladies, who vied with the men of Toledo in giving the party a hearty reception.

On leaving Toledo we left also the delegates from Pittsburg, who returned home from that city. However, we were rejoiced to find that many of our entertainers were to accompany us to Detroit, where, at 3.30 o'clock that afternoon, the special train pulled into the Michigan Central depot. The party were immediately taken in hand by the local reception committee and handed into carriages, and were driven up Jefferson avenue to the Museum of Art, where half an hour was spent in admiring its contents. Repairing then to the Russell House, an opportunity was given to become acquainted with our hosts and hostesses. For three-quarters of an hour the corridors and parlors of the hotel were thronged, and impromptu receptions were in progress on every hand. In one parlor Miss Kate Field was the centre of a group, among whom were Hon. Alfred Russell, Hon. Don. M. Dickinson, Richard Storrs Willis and Mrs. Herman Dey. In other parlors similar coteries were gathered, while the rank and file scattered about and enjoyed themselves as best suited their fancy. At 5.30 o'clock the doors of the dining room were thrown open and the guests filed in. In a few moments the room was transformed into a scene of gaiety unsurpassed. A large representation of Detroit's citizenship was present. Among the invited guests were Mr. and Mrs. Richard Storrs Willis, Mrs.

John J. Bagley, Col. William Ludlow, U. S. A., Mrs. Campau
Thompson, Mrs. Herman Dey, Alfred Russell, ex-Postmaster-
General Dickinson and others.   An hour or so was spent in the
discussion of an elegant menu.   The appetites being finally
appeased, Mr. William E. Quinby, Chairman of the Reception
Committee, rapped for order and called upon the Mendelsohn
Quartet for a vocal selection.   Mr. Quinby then welcomed the
guests and introduced as the first speaker the Hon. Don. M.
Dickinson, ex-Postmaster-General.   Mr. Dickinson, who was greeted
with a round of cheers, expressed a hearty welcome to the visitors
on behalf of the citizens of Detroit.   He paid a handsome tribute
to the ladies of the party, which brought out several "ohs" and
"mys" in different parts of the room.   He thought it would be
well if the ladies always attended banquets, although he could not
sincerely say the men would have a better time if they should.   The
"ahs" were in the majority at this remark.   Mr. Dickinson dwelt
warmly upon the prospects of Detroit as a future seaport.   He
said: "We are to have direct connection with tide-water and, in the
course of time, we will trade direct with Liverpool and the ports
of South America without change of bulk.   We are bound to get
it, and the great Northwest, an empire in itself, will hew and
dig and blast away until we do get it.   The time will come when
we can load our own ships at our doors with provisions for
starving Russia without asking your leave of Congress."   Mr.
Dickinson was succeeded by Delegate T. H. Martin, of Philadelphia,
and Miss Kate Field, of Washington, and the entertainment was
brought to a cheery close by the "Modoes" of the Wagner Buffet
car giving one of their characteristic demoniacal war whoops, after
hearing which no person felt any desire to prolong the sitting
another instant.   But the day's festivities were by no means ended.
Hardly had the banquet hall been vacated when the guests entered

the carriages and were driven to the residence of General R. A.
Alger. Here they were received by General and Mrs. Alger, their
daughters and sons. The elegant home, with its wealth of paintings,
was for more than an hour a brilliant scene. The guests were
continually on the move, and many acquaintances were formed that
will long be treasured by the participants. Among the diversions

VIEW OF NIAGARA FALLS FROM THE CANADIAN SIDE

was a humorous speech of Col. William Ludlow on the "Army
and Navy," and several stories were told by Marshall P. Wilder.
General Alger himself was called upon to speak during the
evening, and responded with graceful eloquence.

At eleven o'clock we took the train again. It was the last

night we were to enjoy its hospitable shelter. With great regret, a sentiment that was experienced on both sides, we took leave here of our *fidus Achates* Jerome, of ever blessed memory. Wearied with the excitements of the day, the party were soon wrapped in slumber, and it seemed as though they had hardly fallen asleep when they were routed out again at seven o'clock on

EMERGING FROM THE HIGHLANDS ON THE NEW YORK CENTRAL R. R.

Sunday, January 31st, to view the beauties of Niagara Falls in its winter garb. Fortified with a hasty cup of coffee they were speedily seated in sleighs and comfortably wrapped in warm robes, were whisked away for an hour's ride, in which they were afforded an excellent sight of the Rapids and the river and the Falls from every advantageous point of view. The spectacle is always impressive, marvelous and grand, at whatever season it is enjoyed, but it must be confessed that its sublimity is somewhat cramped when it is partaken of on an empty stomach. It was interesting on returning to the train to note how, after a hot breakfast had been eaten, the enthusiasm of the party burst forth, afresh, as the cataract itself was destined to do when relieved of its icy fetters and polar ornamentation.

Now, all interest was centered upon reaching home. The party was rapidly diminishing in numbers, and leave-taking was in

NEARING HOME.—HIGH BRIDGE, ON THE HARLEM RIVER.

order. At Syracuse, Rochester and Albany guests and delegates who had joined us there on the outward trip bade us adieu, and by nightfall almost the only remaining occupants of the train were the New York delegation and a few from Boston and Philadelphia. There was one more little social incident to occur. We had been rejoined at Niagara by Mr. Roach, Mr. Underwood, of the Michigan Central, leaving us at that point. When night came and we were rattling down the shore of the Hudson at the rate of about sixty-five miles an hour. Mr. Roach was presented by Mr. Berri, on behalf of the whole delegation, with a set of silver, for which he returned thanks in a neat little response that effectually confirmed his reputation as a ready speaker.

At 10 P. M. we were in the Grand Central depot, at our journey's end.

Brundusium longae finis chartaeque viaeque.

THE trip was ended. It had been one of unalloyed
enjoyment. The party of 120 men and women found
themselves again at their point of departure without
the occurrence of a single mishap to mar the record
of nearly four weeks of pleasurable excitement and
incessant activity. In that interval they had been
carried twice across the breadth of the continent;
had visited all the places of interest on their route;
had received entertainment such as had seldom, if ever before,
been tendered to strangers on the wing, and had, furthermore, in
various ways contributed to the making of history. Not the least
noteworthy of these was the manner in which the details of the
journey had been conducted. In truth, the whole success of the
trip was due to the magnificent provision made for their
entertainment by the officials of the New York Central Railroad
Company conjointly with those of the Wagner Palace Car
Company. The former gave the use of its tracks, and the power
of its potent influence exercised magic sway on every road the
train traveled over. The Wagner Company supplemented this by
tendering to the delegates the most sumptuously appointed and
most profusely stocked special train of vestibuled palace cars that
ever set out from the Grand Central Depot. Every attribute of

comfort, ease and luxurious satisfaction that modern ingenuity has devised for the gratification of the traveling public, was combined in that special train, and, what was more to the purpose, it was there to be used and to be enjoyed to the utmost. The train, composed of six cars, represented the highest development of railway luxury. First was the Buffet smoking car, " No. 655," followed by two sleeping cars, the "Westmoreland" and " Windermere." Then came the dining car in the center of the train. The last two cars were the " Raeburn " and the "Magenta," the latter being divided into state-room compartments. The whole train was warmed with steam and Baker heaters, and lighted by gas, though there was prudently an abundance of auxiliary oil and bracket candle lamps, to be used when the gas gave out. Each car was supplied with hot and cold water. The interiors were upholstered to correspond with the wood work with silk damask, bordered with plush. It was claimed to be the heaviest solid vestibule train that ever made the round trip between New York and San Francisco. At every station where it stopped it excited the greatest admiration and praise, and the loudest of all to proclaim its beauty and magnificence were the railroad men, who flocked to the depots to inspect it. Nothing that skill and enterprise could devise was lacking in its equipment, and it was complacently claimed by the travelers that it was superior to the train which shortly before had conveyed President Harrison's party on its trip to the Pacific coast. The Wagner people determined that the newspaper men should have no possible chance for adverse criticism, and they carried their intentions out to the very letter. The only reasonable criticism the guests could conjure up was based upon the lavish character of their entertainment. A more efficient crew of attendants never accompanied a train. Every man knew his business and, therefore, every want of the passengers was cared for. There were in all twenty employés, consisting of the conductor, steward, barber, four cooks, five waiters, six porters and the baggagemen. In regard to the cooking there was nothing left to be desired, and from the first day that the party dined on the outward journey to the return to New York there was no room for the slightest complaint. The service on the part of the steward, Mr. E. L. Cornell, and his efficient aids would challenge comparison with that of the best hotels in the United States. The favorite resort of the gentlemen, particularly the unmarried ones, on the trip was the buffet smoker. It was a thing of beauty and a joy, and without it the pleasure of the trip would have been immeasureably lessened. This traveling club-house was finished in oak and mahogany. The forward part was used for baggage. Next came a bath-room, and adjoining the bath was the barber's room, containing a barber's chair, in which, thanks to the skill of Mr. Frank, the tonsorial artist who presided, the requirements of the travelers in his line could be attended to with almost as much satisfaction at a forty mile gait, as under the most favorable conditions in a barber shop on *terra firma*. Next to the barber shop were two sections that could be used for card playing. I do not state that they were so utilized, however. These two sections could be entirely shut off from the other portions of the car by means of a mahogany partition and plush curtains. Back of this adjustable section was a writing desk, furnished with stationery on tap, and all the conveniences for correspondence or telegraphing, while on the other side, Mr. W. Archer, the stenographer from Mr. Yager's New York office, with his writing machine, was located. His services were placed at the disposal of the travelers, and were in steady requisition. The central portion of the buffet car was devoted to the smokers. Here there were large moveable easy chairs of oak and cane, heavily upholstered with plush. "Standing room only," was almost invariably the condition in this part of the train after meals and during the evening. Long will the remembrance abide of the funny stories, the racy anecdotes, the recitations, the shop talk, the schemes of organization, the earnest debates and the hot-headed discussions, as well as the effervescences of high-flown rhetoric, and the bursts of eloquence that were steadily in progress in that buffet car during the trip. Neither will the war whoop of "the Modoes" be readily forgotten. Next in order came the most extensively patronized of all the special departments of the train. This was the buffet itself, from which the rubicund Dan, or his sober-minded companion Gates, incessantly peered, awaiting calls for lemonade, ginger ale, sarsaparilla and soda, or occasionally the foaming beer bottle. There, also, was a library of admirably selected books, which served to beguile many a leisure hour to all the passengers on the train. Next to the buffet car was the Westmoreland, the "Stag Car" as it was designated, being occupied exclusively by the bachelors of the party. In the other cars were the married delegates and the ladies and other guests. The dining car was one of the hand-somest ever constructed, and, of course, of the most approved pattern, the old style of section seats having been superseded by the substitution of chairs. On the left side of the car, as the illustration shows, were tables accommodating four persons, and on the right side there were tables seating two each, thus giving ample room for passing back and forth. Thirty persons could be served at one time. What added greatly to the convenience and enjoyment of the trip was the circumstance already alluded to, that all the tables in the car could be removed and a change could be made into a traveling hall, where frequent entertain-ments were given during the trip.

The guests of the trip were attentively cared for. Mrs. Frank Leslie occupied a drawing-room section in the Raeburn, and was very comfortably situated. Mr. Willie Wilde occupied a section to himself, just outside. Miss Kate Field was assigned a state-room in the last car of the train—the Magenta—in which car were most of the officers of the League and their wives and invited guests. This car was one of particularly elegant construction and convenience, the state-rooms being so arranged that they could, if desired, be joined in suites.

Despite the size and weight of this great train, it arrived at its destination half an hour ahead of its schedule time, and this in the face of the severe storms that accompanied it in its entire trip from New York to San Francisco. It is a remarkable fact that there was not a hot box during the whole journey, though the brake-shoes were almost worn through on account of the enormous and arduous amount of work done on the heavy grades over the Rockies and Sierras. "There were served," says Statistician Morse, of the Boston Press Club, "about 125 people per day. The train was provisioned at New York with groceries, etc., for the round trip, while perishable supplies were purchased en route. The train was equipped, in addition to other essential articles, with 1,000 sheets, 1,000 slips, 2,500 hand towels, 500 barber towels, 50 glass towels, 500 table cloths, 1,500 napkins and 650 doylies. The expense of the washing for the trip was over $400, laundry work having to be done at San Bernardino and San Francisco. Everything was as bright and clean and as fresh on the return to New York as had been the case at the departure."

That everything was so admirably contrived for the enjoyment of the whole trip, was in a very large measure due to the executive abilities and energetic efforts of Messrs. W. B. Jerome,

DINING CAR IN THE PENN THE EARLY SIXTIES, WESTBOUND

General Western Passenger Agent of the New York Central Railroad, and Mr. J. C. Yager, the Eastern Superintendent of the Wagner Palace Car Company. Mr. Jerome was the railway representative on the entire trip from Chicago, and the manner in which he attended to his portion of the duties called forth the highest praise from every member of the party. Mr. Jerome is a native of Auburn, N. Y., and has occupied his present responsible position about ten years.

The excellence of the internal economy of the train and the service and discipline were due to the presence of Superintendent of the Wagner Palace Car Company John C. Yager. That gentleman made it a point to anticipate the wants of every one on the train, and any suggestion that came to his ears received instant attention. He seemed to be omnipresent. He omitted nothing. He watched everything. Mr. Yager was born in Piqua, Ohio, and has been connected with sleeping car companies for the past sixteen years, during seven of which he has occupied the position of Eastern Superintendent for the Wagner Company, having charge of all lines east of Buffalo, with headquarters at New York.

Another railway official who left no stone unturned to secure for the delegates the unprecedented comfort that they enjoyed, and who succeeded admirably therein, was Mr. Milton C. Roach, General Eastern Passenger Agent of the New York Central and Hudson River Railroad. Mr. Roach not only accompanied the party as far as Chicago, but also delighted the many friends that he made on the outward trip by returning from Niagara Falls to New York with them.

To Mr. George H. Daniels, of the New York Central Railroad, is due a large share of credit, for it was he who made it possible for his subordinates to perform their work so well, and

138

GUESTS AND RAILROAD OFFICIALS.

Dr. A. S. Hunter,	J. Seaver Page,	M. H. Brown,
W. B. Jerome.	M. C. Roach.	J. C. Yager.

it was he who made all the preliminary arrangements for the journey, that resulted in such wholesale success. Mr. E. J. Richards, Assistant General Passenger Agent, was also solicitious for our welfare, accompanying the party to Albany on the outward trip, and meeting it again on the return, to escort it through New York State to its starting point.

Nothing, in fact, could surpass the watchful care with which the Eastern travelers were unremittingly surrounded by their railroad hosts and protectors. Up the mountains and down the mountains, through narrow and precipitous passes, past craggy ledges and by the edges of rivers the train was borne along at sometimes startling speed, but the passengers were relieved from all sense of nervousness by the knowledge that their immediate destinies were in the charge of the Napoleonic Jerome, unruffled, alert, unsleeping, all observant, and always thoroughly master of the situation. If the journey, in all its perfect details, realized the notion of "the poetry of travel," Jerome was the poet laureate to whom was due the even smoothness that marked its cadenced rhythm. Then, too, over each road that was traversed the party was escorted by some of its highest officials. The narrative of the journey would be incomplete without a detailed record of the gentlemen who accompanied the delegates over the lines of road they severally represented, and to whom the travelers desire, through this medium, to express their earnest thanks. They were:

J. C. YAGER, Division Superintendent of the Wagner Palace Car Company, representing his company on the entire trip (accompanied by Mrs. Yager).

W. B. JEROME, General Western Passenger Agent of the New York Central and Hudson River Railroad, representing his company the entire trip from Chicago to San Francisco, and returning, to Detroit.

E. J. RICHARDS, Assistant General Passenger Agent New York Central Railroad, from New York to Albany.

M. C. ROACH, General Eastern Passenger Agent, New York Central Railroad, New York to Chicago, and return from Niagara Falls.

W. H. UNDERWOOD, Eastern Passenger Agent, Michigan Central Railroad, New York to Chicago, and Detroit to Buffalo on return.

C. L. LEONORI, General Commissary, Wagner Palace Car Company, Buffalo to Chicago.

JAMES GIBSON, District Passenger Agent, Chicago and Northwestern Railway, Chicago to Omaha.

B. S. ANDREWS, of the Passenger and Ticket Department, Chicago and Northwestern Railway, Chicago to Denver.

D. E. BURLEY, of the Passenger Department, Union Pacific Railway, Omaha to Denver.

S. K. HOOPER, General Passenger and Ticket Agent, Denver and Rio Grande Railroad, Denver to Salt Lake.

F. A. WADLEIGH, Assistant General Passenger Agent, Denver and Rio Grande Railroad, Denver to Grand Junction.

J. J. BURNS, Superintendent of First Division, Denver and Rio Grande Railroad, Colorado Springs to Glenwood Springs.

C. C. SMITH, Assistant General Passenger Agent, Rio Grande Western Railway, Grand Junction to Ogden.

W. L. KNIGHT, Traveling Passenger Agent, Southern Pacific Railway, Ogden to San Francisco and Los Angeles.

W. C. MORROW, of the Passenger Department, Southern Pacific Railway, Ogden to San Francisco and Los Angeles.

E. F. BURNETT, Passenger Agent, Atchison, Topeka and Santa Fé Railroad, from Los Angeles to Kansas City, Mo.

F. CHANDLER, General Passenger and Ticket Agent, Wabash Railroad Company, Kansas City to Detroit.

H. DURAND, Passenger Department, Wabash Railroad Company, Kansas City to St. Louis.

This record of our railroad hosts should include the names of Dr. Seward Webb, President, and Mr. C. D. Flagg, Vice-President of the Wagner Palace Car Company, who directed that the special Wagner train be placed at the disposal of the League and made the agreeable trip possible.

Railroad officials deserving of most honorable and grateful mention, besides those named above, are, Mr. O. W. Ruggles, General Passenger and Ticket Agent, Michigan Central Railroad ; Mr. W. F. White, Passenger Traffic Manager, Atchison, Topeka

& Santa Fé Railroad Company, and Mr. C. P. Huntington, President Southern Pacific Company.

A further illustration of the solicitude shown for the Press Club party by their railroad entertainers was afforded in the circumstance of their inviting Dr. Alexander S. Hunter, one of New York's distinguished physicians, to take part in the trip, in the capacity of special medical attendant. Dr. Hunter was accompanied by his estimable wife. His own genial presence was a continuous tonic and stimulant, and possibly to the confidence imparted by that attractive quality on his part was due the unusual fact of a party of over a hundred persons making a continued journey of nearly nine thousand miles without any one of the number falling sick or in any serious way requiring medical attendance.

In fact, the personnel of the party was, throughout, all that could have been desired to render the trip a success. The subject must not be closed without mentioning the attendance on the route of a phantom guest, who turned up regularly at every stopping place, and was a welcome participant in the

H. W. CHAPIN, OF SYRACUSE.

entertainments provided for the travelers, disappearing, however, as soon as preparations began for resuming the journey. This mysterious traveling companion was Mr. H. W. Chapin, of Syracuse, a popular member of the Press Club of that city. By careful study and manipulation of the time tables, Mr. Chapin managed to secure a train just in advance of the "Wagner special," so as to be regularly on hand to welcome the party on its arrival at each successive point where it was to disembark from the train. He had the remarkable fortune in a trip of 9,153 miles to make every connection that he had planned before setting out from Syracuse, though he confessed afterward that it had kept him very busy to keep pace with the rapid movements of the Wagner excursionists.

———

Travel has been declared to be the " Fool's Paradise." If the epigram embodies a truth, it is also true that the fool may inhabit Paradise without monopolizing it. It would be a narrow and imperfect view of the subject that would seek to belittle the gratification of travel or to exclude men of sense from its appreciative enjoyment. A man may make a journey of many miles in these days of rails and wires without really slackening his grasp upon the interests he leaves behind him, nor can he fairly consider himself as ever getting wholly out of reaching distance of his home. The improvements in this respect which have occurred within the observation of men still in the prime of life are among the most striking illustrations of the accelerated velocity with which this moribund Nineteenth Century has been spinning " down the ringing grooves of change." There are many who readily recall the time when a voyage to Europe, or especially a trip across this continent, was a portentous undertaking, demanding serious contemplation beforehand, and perhaps exciting the sympathetic apprehensions of one's acquaintances. Who shall dare to conjecture what facilities for traveling will be in use at the end of the next century? But let them be what they may, with all their possibilities of improved conditions, they cannot confer greater satisfaction upon the people of that coming period than the Press Club Leaguers of this day and generation experienced in their rapid railroad ride briefly related in the preceding pages. The narrative has been prepared at the request of the League, merely to give enduring form to the recollection of what must be treasured as an enjoyable episode in the life of every man and woman who took part in it. It was not desired, on the one hand, nor attempted on the other, to make this more than a condensed recital of such incidents as fell within the writer's own observation, and, accordingly, he has not aimed at describing those facts from the high standpoint of expert reporting, nor on the lower plane of editorial discussion. As Martial says: "His subject was so fruitful that he had the less need for the exercise of wit."

Appendix.

Route of Travel of the International Press League.

New York Central and Michigan Central— MILES.
New York to Chicago.................................. 976

Chicago and Northwestern—
Chicago to Omaha......... 503

Union Pacific—
Omaha to Denver... 572

Denver and Rio Grande and Rio Grande Western—
Denver to Ogden.. 784

Side Trips about Salt Lake City and to Gas Wells..................... 35

Southern Pacific—
Ogden to San Francisco.... 895
San Francisco to Monterey..... 127
Monterey to Pajaro.. 28
Pajaro to Santa Cruz... 21
Santa Cruz to San Jose.... 35
San Jose to San Francisco.................................... 50
San Francisco to Los Angeles......... 482

Southern California (now A., T. and S. F. R. R.)—
Los Angeles to Pasedena and Return....... 20
Los Angeles to Redondo Beach and return....................... 46
Los Angeles to Redlands and return to San Bernardino........... 71
San Bernardino to San Diego.................................. 124

Atchison, Topeka and Santa Fé—
San Diego to Kansas City, making stops as follows : Albuquerque,
Santa Fé and Las Vegas Hot Springs........................ 2,392
Lamy Junction to Santa Fé and return.......................... 36
Las Vegas to Hot Springs and return........ 12

Wabash Railroad—
Kansas City to St. Louis. 277
St. Louis to Toledo. 436

Michigan Central Railway—
Toledo to Detroit.. .. 59
Detroit to Buffalo.... 251

New York Central Railroad—
Buffalo to New York..................... 444

Total 8,676

What the Delegates Had to Say About the Trip.

The subjoined list of the special contributions sent to their respective papers during the journey by the delegates on the train is not claimed to be exhaustive. It comprises those only which have come before the notice of the present writer. The dates given are those of their publication:

Chas. W. Price, *Electrical Review*—
    Feb. 13th. "The Press Club League Convention."

J. C. Morse, Boston *Herald*—
    Feb. 3d. "The Press Delegates' Train."

J. B. Dampman, Reading *Herald*—
    Jan. 9th. "The Start and the Train."
    " 13th. "On the Fly through Nebraska."
    " 16th. "Denver's Magic Growth."
    " 19th. "Crossing the Rockies."
    " 20th. "Salt Lake City."
    " 25th. "At the Golden Gate."
    " 26th. "California's Wonders."
    " 29th. "Model Street Cars in San Francisco."
    " 30th. "Vineyards of Fresno."
    Feb. 1st. "San José."
    " 2d. "A Visit to Monterey."
    " 3d. "Receptions and Banquets."
    " 5th. "Sacramento to Los Angeles."
    " 2d. "Banquet of the Reading Press Club."

C. H. George, Baltimore *American*—
    Feb. 5th. "From Ocean to Ocean."

* Miss Mary Allen West, Chicago *Union Signal*-
    "Across the Continent."

T. J. Keenan, Jr., Pittsburgh *Press*—
    Feb. 11th. "Over the Rockies."
    " 15th. "Salt Lake and Auburn."
    " 20th. "Chinatown."

* This most estimable lady, a distinguished temperance advocate, separated from the party at Los Angeles to visit Japan on missionary work, and died in Tokyo, December 1st, '92.

148

T. J. Keenan, Jr., Pittsburgh *Press*—
  Feb. 22d. "Monterey, etc., etc."
  " 23d. "Southern California."
  Mch. 6th. "The Homeward Trip."
  " 16th. "The Journey's End."

W. V. Alexander, Boston *Transcript*—
  Feb. 13th. "From Ocean to Ocean."

Lynn R. Meekins, Baltimore *American*—
  Feb. 12th. "From Snow to Flowers."
  " 14th. "A Day in Mormondom." (2)
  Mch. 12th. "Through New Mexico."
  "A Week in California."

Mrs. E. M. Avery, Cleveland *Leader*—
  Jan. 25th. "A Glorious Time."
              (Chicago to San Francisco.)
           "Across the Desert."

E. H. O'Hara, Syracuse—
  Feb. 13th. "Some Things that I Saw."

M. P. Murphy, Toledo *Bee*—
  Jan. 30th. "Reception in Toledo."
  Feb. 1st. "Incidents of the Tour."

E. J. Fleming, Buffalo *Express*—
           "Across the Continent."

J. S. Keeler, Boston *Herald*—
  Jan. 26th. "Sight-Seeing on the Pacific Coast (San José).
  Feb. 1st, "Doing Lower California."
  " 7th. "Incidents of Interest."
  " 21st. "Further Incidents."
  " 28th. "A Boston Delegate in Chinatown."
  Mch. 13th. "The Heart of Chinatown."
  " 27th. "The Land of the Setting Sun."

Mrs. Frances E. Owens, Chicago *Journal of Industrial Education*—
              February, March and April.

Irving Watson, Narragansett *Herald*—

Mrs. Kate F. McElrath, *American Analyst*, New York—
  Feb. 25th. "Atlantic to Pacific."
  Mch. 3d. " "

Miss Belle Gorton, Chicago *Woman's News*—
  Feb. 13th. "Across the Continent."
  " 20th. "In California."

Miss Belle Gorton, Chicago *Woman's News*—

    Mch. 5th.   "
    " 12th.   "
    " 26th.   "

Kate Field's *Washington*—

    Jan. 13th. "International League of Press Clubs."
    Mch. 9th. "Crossing the Continent."
    " 16th. "Denver."
    " 23d. "Omaha and Palmer Lake."
    April 6th. "Glenwood Springs and Zion."
    " 13th. "Pioneers and Nevada."

W. N. Penney, New York *News*—

    Feb. 14th. "A Sunday Amid the Rockies."
    " 21st. "Sunday Among the Palms."
    " 28th. "Sunday in Semi-Tropical Seas."
    Mch. 6th. "Sunday on the Road—Niagara."

Julius Muehle, *Der Seebote*, Milwaukee, Wis.—

    Feb. 3d. "To California."
    " 6th. "The League Convention."
    " 11th. "Southern California."

T. P. McElrath, *American Analyst*, New York—

    Feb. 18th. "Convention of Press Clubs."

E. B. Fisher, Grand Rapids, Mich., *Eagle*—

    Jan. 17th. "The Press Excursion."
    " 24th. "From the Coast."
    " 31st. "Some Rare Experiences."
    Feb. 7th. "The Great Wonder of It."

William Berri, Brooklyn *Standard-Union*—

    Feb. 1st. "Across the Continent and Back."

www.ingramcontent.com/pod-product-compliance
Lightning Source LLC
Chambersburg PA
CBHW030558270326
41927CB00007B/980